~ Dedication ~

For Paula Scully, who has encouraged me every step of the way,
and for Sam, who steps in when I need him the most.
Thanks so very much for your support!

TABLE of CONTENTS

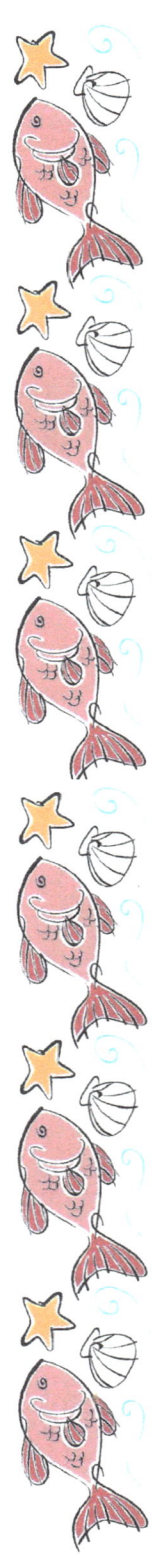
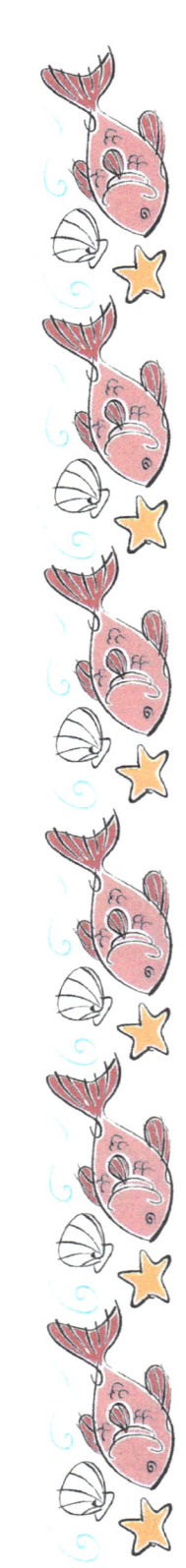

Zentangle® Creativity & You

It's my (humble) opinion that **everyone** has a spark of creativity in them. Whether it means you're able to design a house, knit a scarf, draw stick people, or color pictures; whatever the spark is, we each have our very own form of creativity. If that creativity was never nourished, or encouraged, is another matter. Consider this... it's never too late to find your creative niche.

As a Certified Zentangle Teacher (CZT), I've heard so many students remark, "This is just another type of doodling." If that's their take on this delightful art form, they're welcome to it. ☺ For me, Zentangle is *more* directed, *more* focused, *more* relaxing, and *more* mindful. Best of all... it's **more** creative for everyone who takes the opportunity to tangle.

Rick Roberts & Maria Thomas began this craze and have given much to their students through the certification classes they host in Providence, RI. They are generous and wonderfully gifted people.

I've been an artist in one form or another for most of my life. Decorative painting was my main interest until I stepped outside the proverbial box and took a class in Zentangle. After taking two classes, with a CZT, I registered for certification with Rick Roberts and Maria Thomas. Tangling is the best thing I've found to enhance the art of relaxation, ease stress, control anxiety, to recharge my energy levels, increase confidence, and the list goes on. It may sound too good to be true, but I guarantee you can benefit from Zentangle too, as long as you take some time to tangle. ♥

Find more information on Zentangle®, at www.zentangle.com
To visit my blog, go to www.zenoftangling.blogspot.com

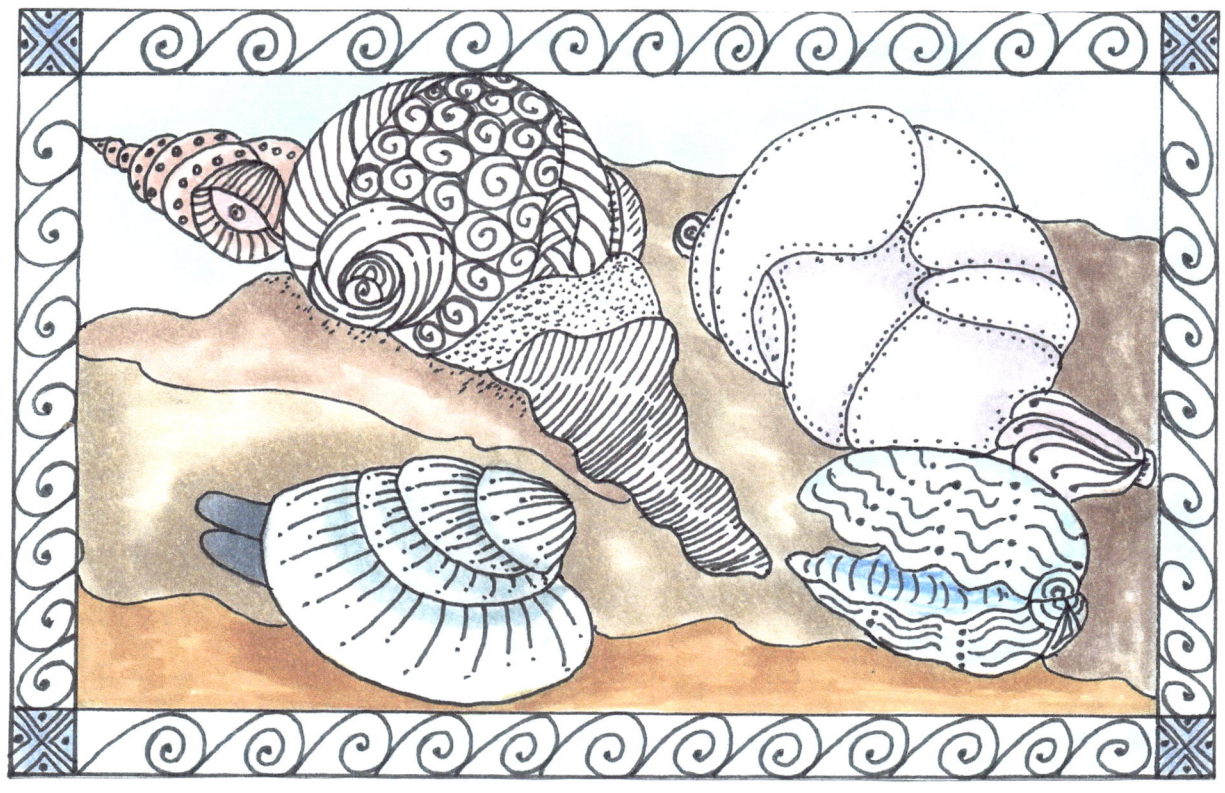

Creative Materials used in Zentangle by the Sea:

A host of supplies will be used in this book. For example, we'll try out several papers, rubber stamps, pens, various pencils, types of markers, gelatos, and more. Here are a few samples done using some of these materials.

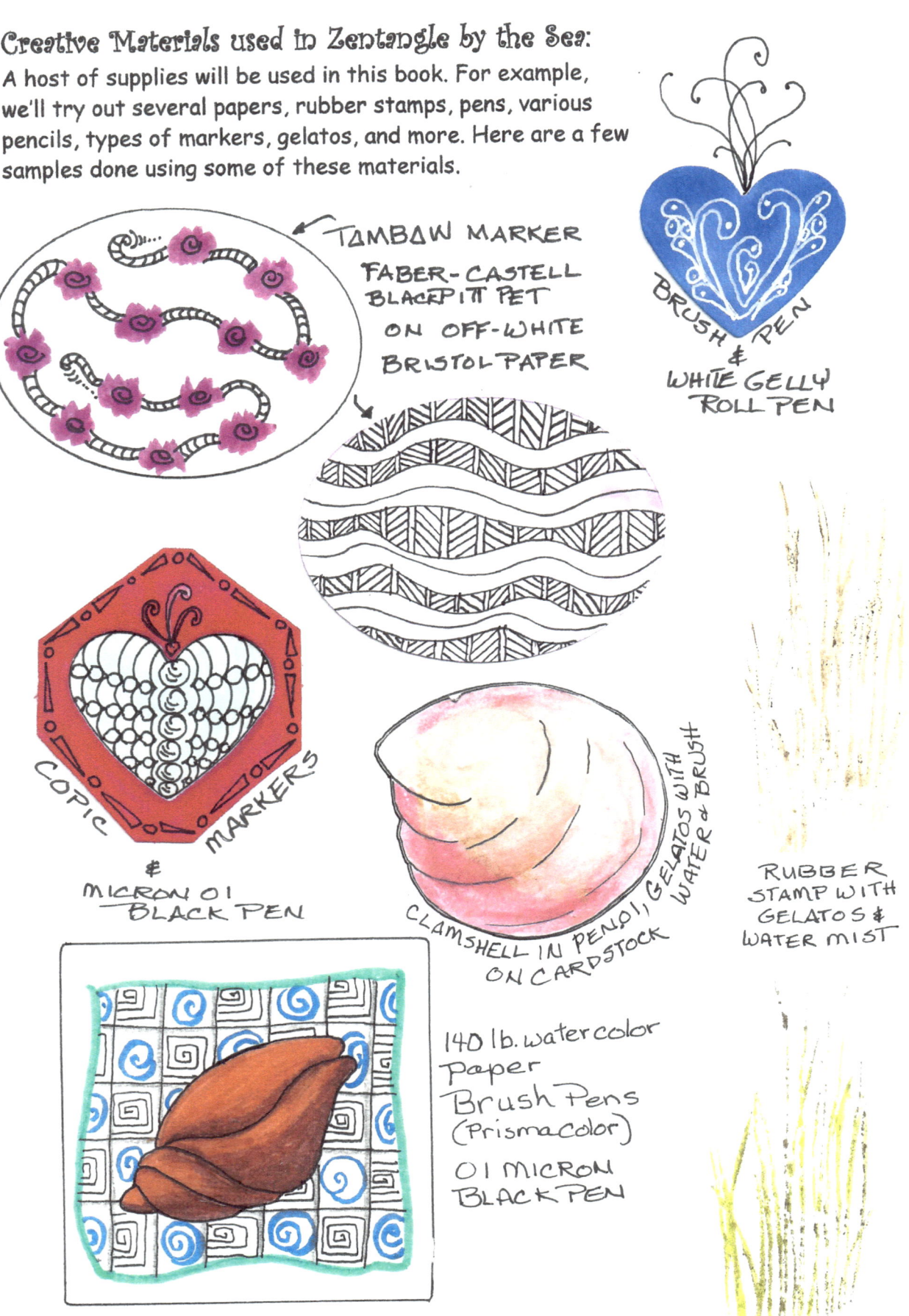

TAMBOW MARKER
FABER-CASTELL
BLACEPITT PET
ON OFF-WHITE
BRISTOL PAPER

BRUSH PEN
&
WHITE GELLY
ROLL PEN

COPIC MARKERS
&
MICRON 01
BLACK PEN

CLAMSHELL IN PENCIL, GELATOS WITH WATER & BRUSH
ON CARDSTOCK

RUBBER
STAMP WITH
GELATOS &
WATER MIST

140 lb. watercolor
Paper
Brush Pens
(Prismacolor)
01 MICRON
BLACK PEN

RUBBER STAMP
WITH TAMBOW MARKERS

TOOLS OF THE TRADE

Let's talk about pencils. A plain No. 2 pencil is great for shading, but when looking for a light graphite, it's better to get into an **H** type of pencil. H pencils have hard lead that offer a lighter line which is easy to erase. If darker and softer lead is required, go with **B** lead. **B** pencils are soft and dark, any **B** lead (2,4,6, etc.) will offer shading and blending ability that isn't available in **H** type lead.

In Zentangle, shading is done with a soft lead, such as a B lead, or No. 2 lead pencil. The darker the shading, the higher the B lead number is. For instance, **B6** (or higher) lead is very buttery, soft, and blendable on paper, (messy, too, but we can't have everything). ☺

This page is filled with designs that have been shaded with B leads noted next to each tangle.

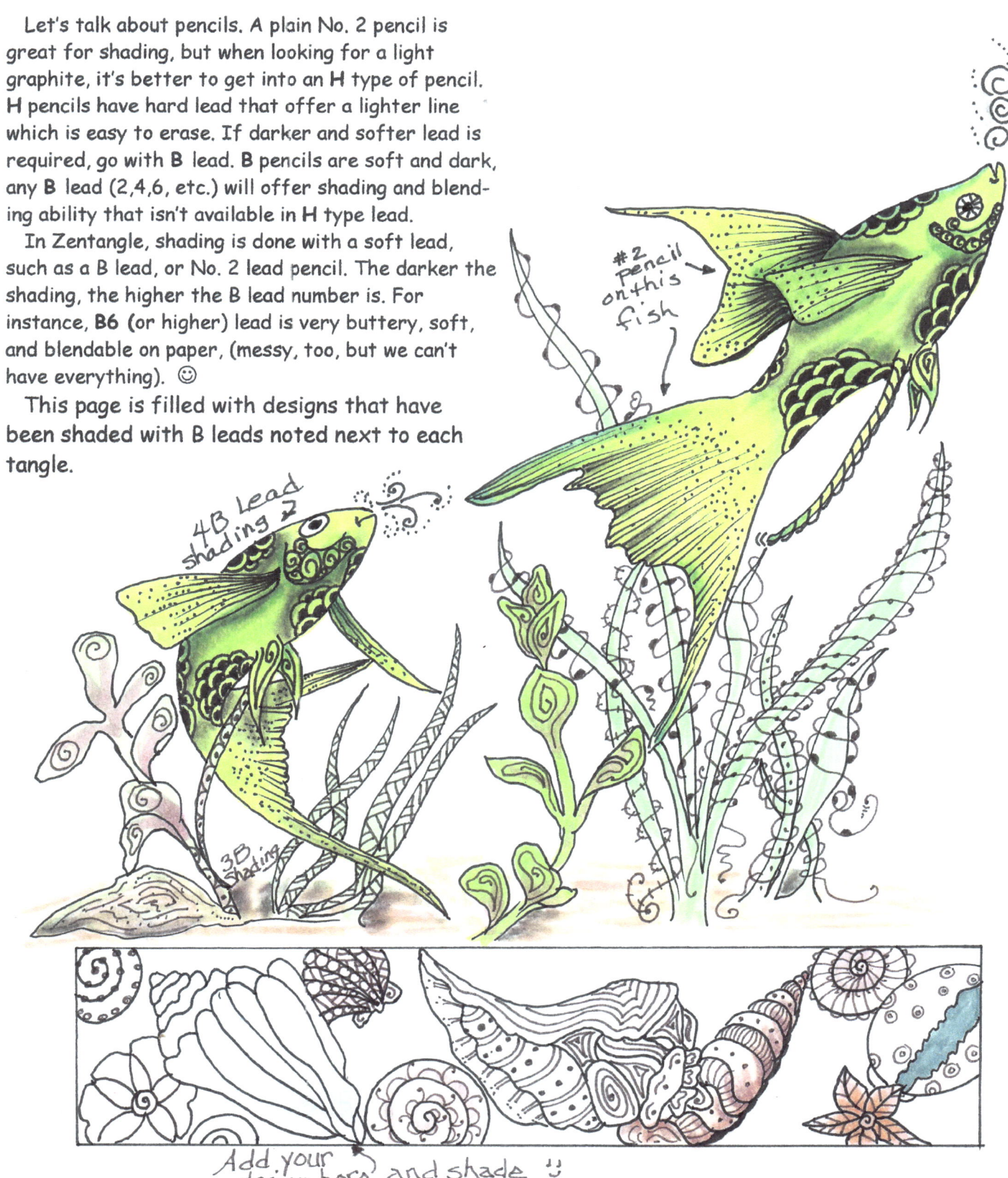

#2 pencil on this fish

4B lead shading 2

3B shading

Add your design here and shade ☺

Pens... Not all pens are created equal. Where they can be found?

To me, shopping for art supplies is what shopping for clothes is to others. I'd rather have art supplies than new shoes or an outfit, anytime! ☺

One of my favorite stores to shop at is Michael's. The store carries a great line of pens, paint, markers, and pencils. I just bought a box set of gelatos there. A.C. Moore or Hobby Lobby are great places to find art or craft supplies, too.

If you don't live near craft stores, or it's too far to just get in the car and run out for this or that, consider shopping online. If you live in a rural area, like I do, sometimes the shipping is cheaper than the cost of gasoline.

For things I can't readily find, I shop online at sites like Dick Blick, Faber-Castell, JoAnn Fabrics, Stampendous, and the Carpe Diem Store (Copic markers are reasonable there). They can all be accessed online.

Pen tip widths offer thin to thick lines. Brush pens (a new love of mine) are nice for coloring or writing fancy letters, etc. Prismacolor makes a superb set in varied line weights such as 02, 03, 04, etc. Check them out, buy one pen, and try it before investing in a full set.

Gelato sampling:

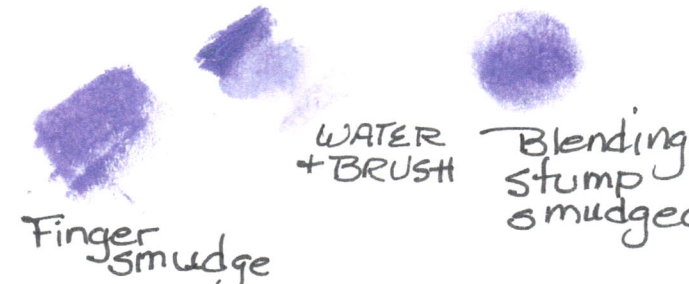

WATER + BRUSH   Blending stump smudged

Finger smudge

Pencil weights: F   B   2B   3B   4B   5B

HB = #2   H   2H   3H   4H   5

Pen tip widths:

005 ///   01 ≡   05 ///   03 ≡

Pen brush: 〰〰〰   〰〰〰

Copic Markers: Brush tip   broad tip:

PROJECTS

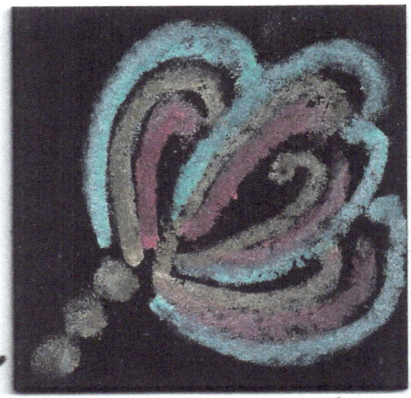

Gelatos Metallics on black inchie, smudged with a blending stump.

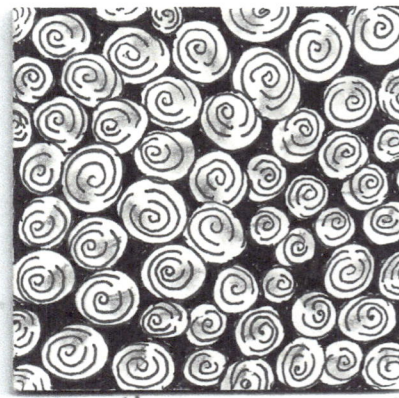

Sea Shells - ∆R
PRINTEMPS ®
005 pen
#2 Pencil for shading.
03 pen for filling.

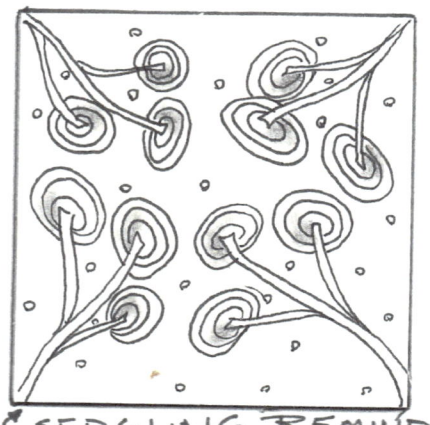

⟵ SEDGLING REMINDS ME OF sea anemones 01 PEN & #2 PENCIL

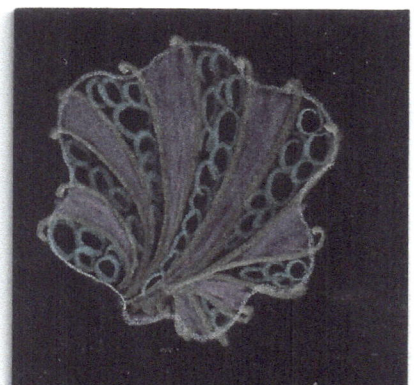

⟵ AQUAFLEUR

DONE WITH METALLIC COLORED PENCIL

NOTICE THE SHELL SHAPE OF IT. ☺

Color Techniques, Adding Color and all that jazz...

  This and the next few pages hold examples of blended gelatos, Copic markers, Tombow markers on rubber stamps, colored pencils, inktense pencils, watercolor pencils, and pastel pencils.

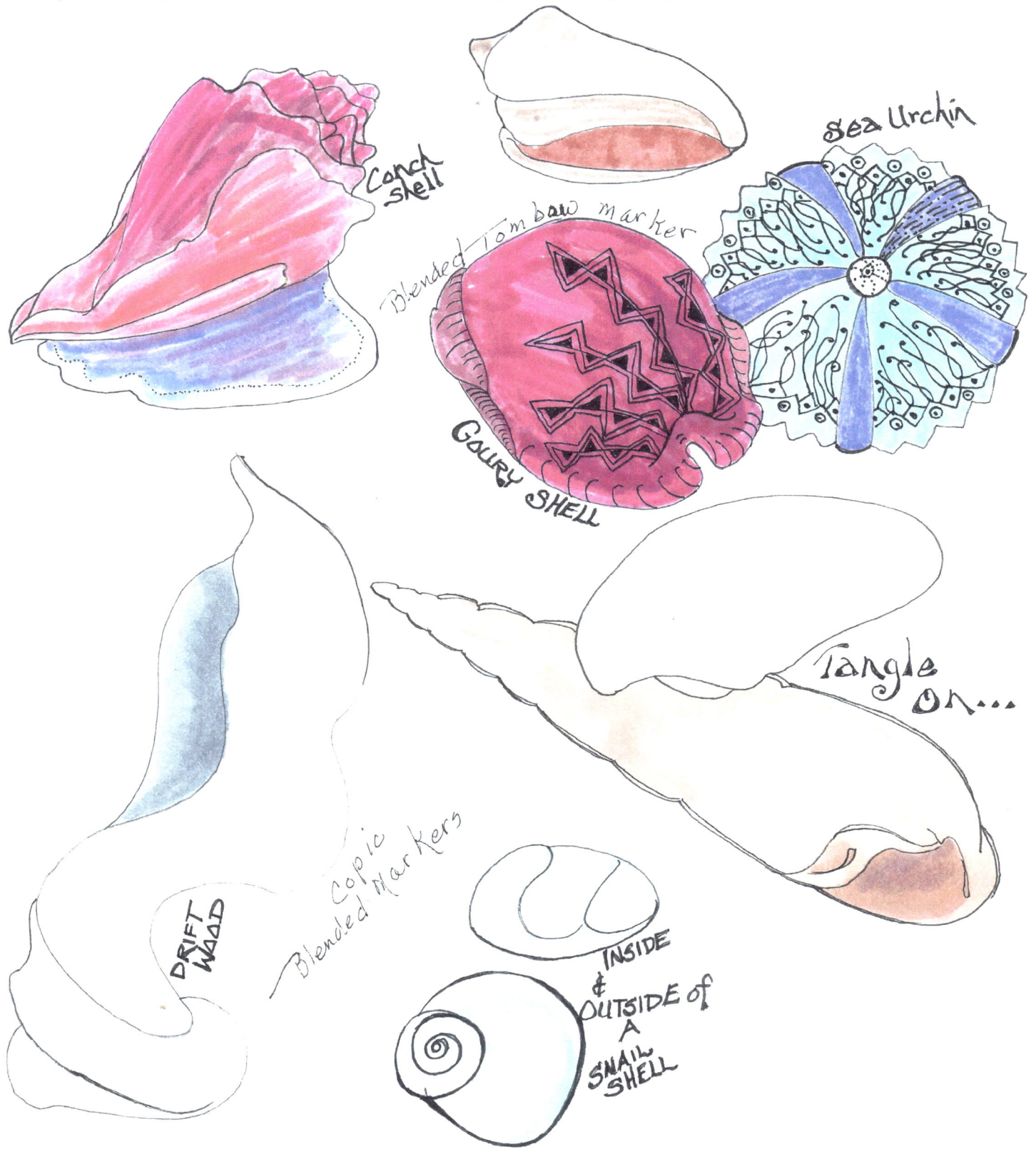

Conch Shell

Sea Urchin

Blended Tombow marker

COWRY SHELL

DRIFT WOOD

Copic Blended Markers

INSIDE & OUTSIDE OF A SNAIL SHELL

Tangle On...

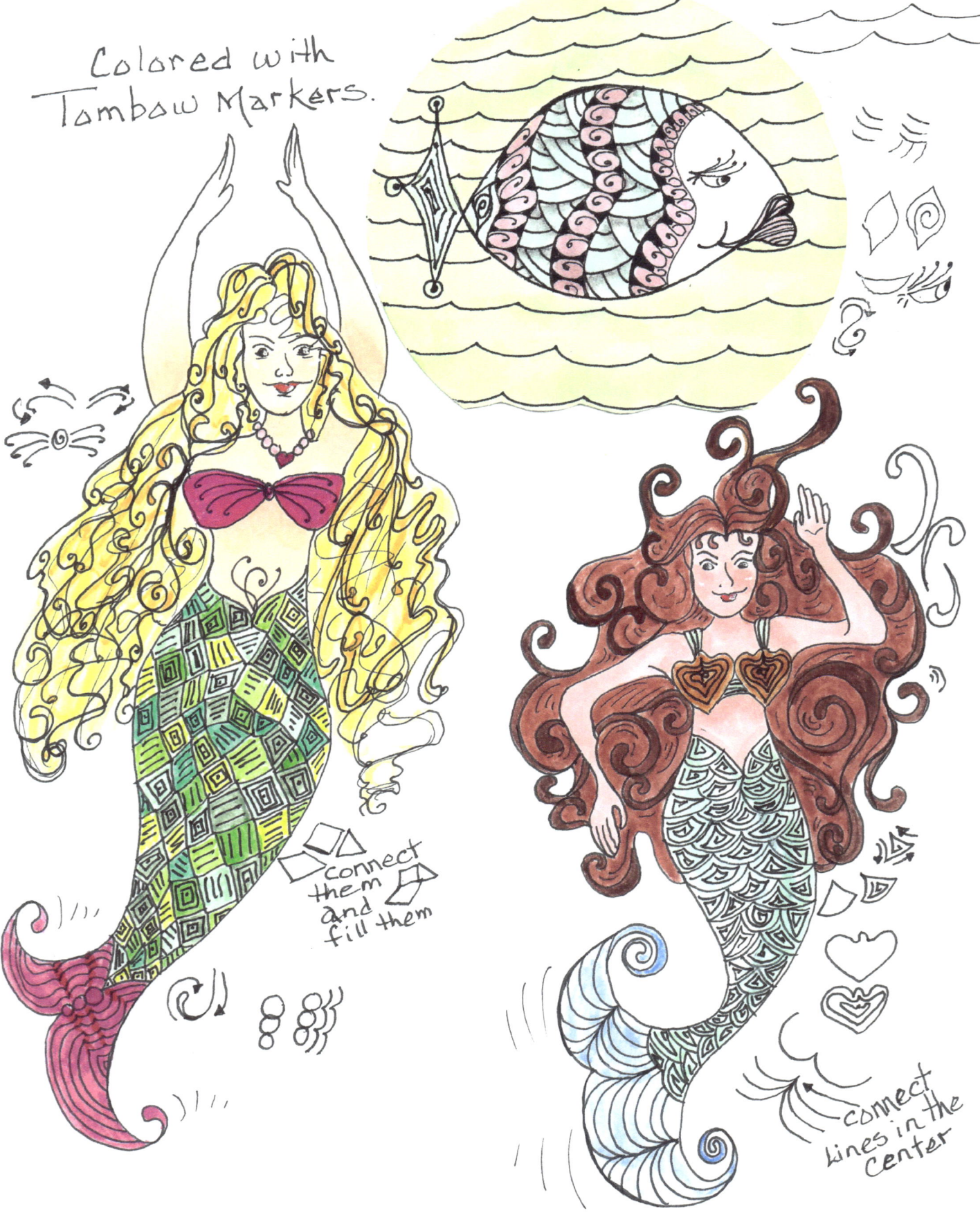

Colored with Tombow Markers.

connect them and fill them

connect lines in the center

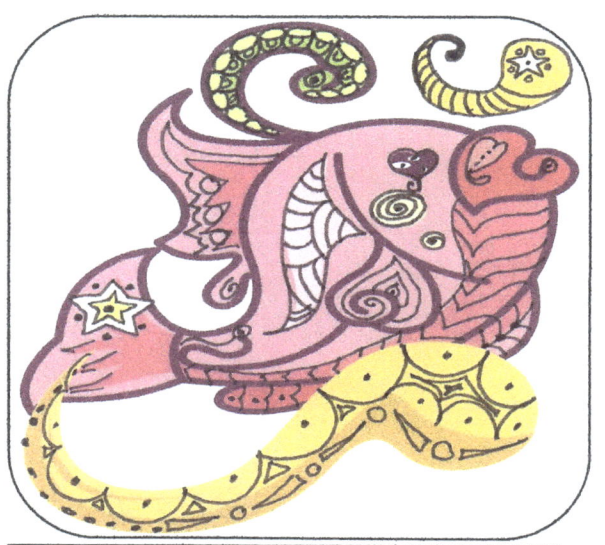

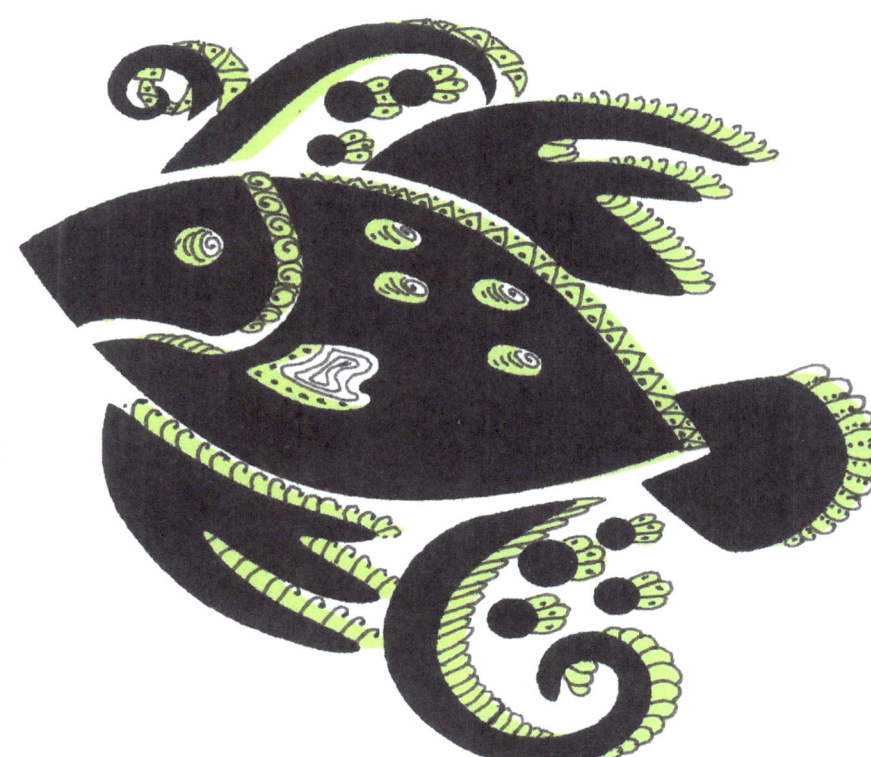

Sea creatures and fish can be fun and simple. Caricatures are especially fun to tangle. Shapes and form are of more importance, this way there are borders to use as a guide.

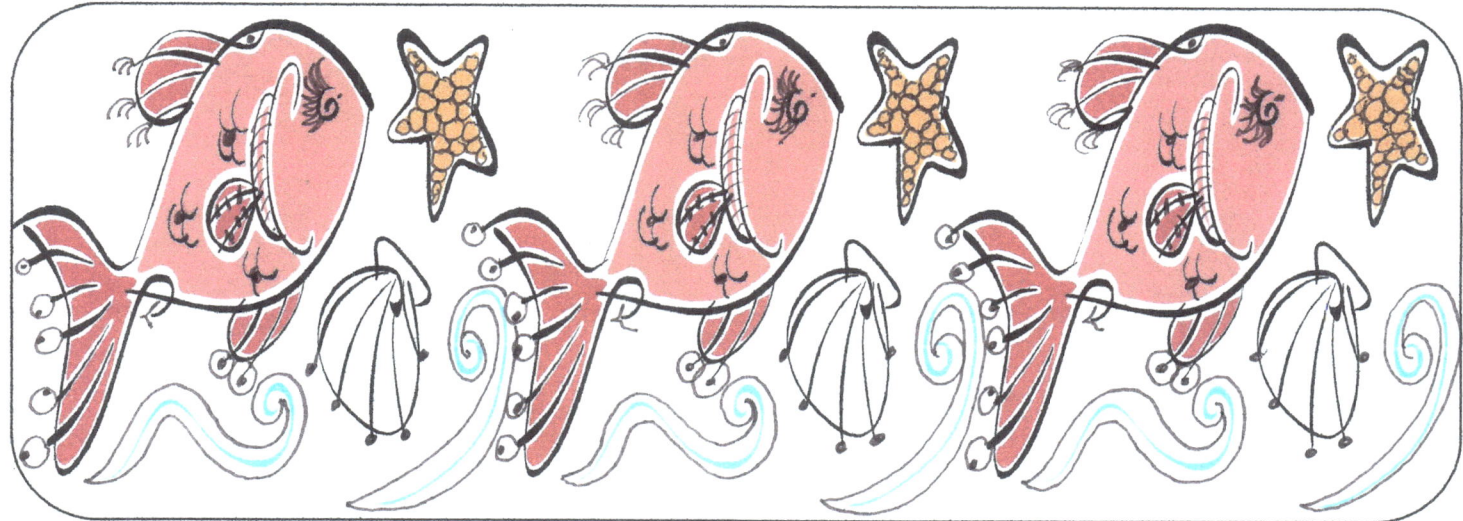

What's in a brand name, you might ask? Brand names often become continuous purchases, or in this instance, continual studio purchases. I use **Copic** markers, **Tombow** markers or those made by **Prismacolor** with others made by **Faber-Castell**. All have their own uniqueness and various methods for usage, but as with all of us, I have preferences.

For instance, I like to use Tombow for stamping, while I find Copics marvelous for coloring and blending. Faber-Castell makes wonderful gelatos, which can be used in many different ways. Prismacolor brush markers are great, as are their colored pencils, which go on paper like soft butter, and are fun to use. Gel pens by **Sakura** are a favorite of mine, as well. When shopping, try to buy quality products, it pays off in the long run.

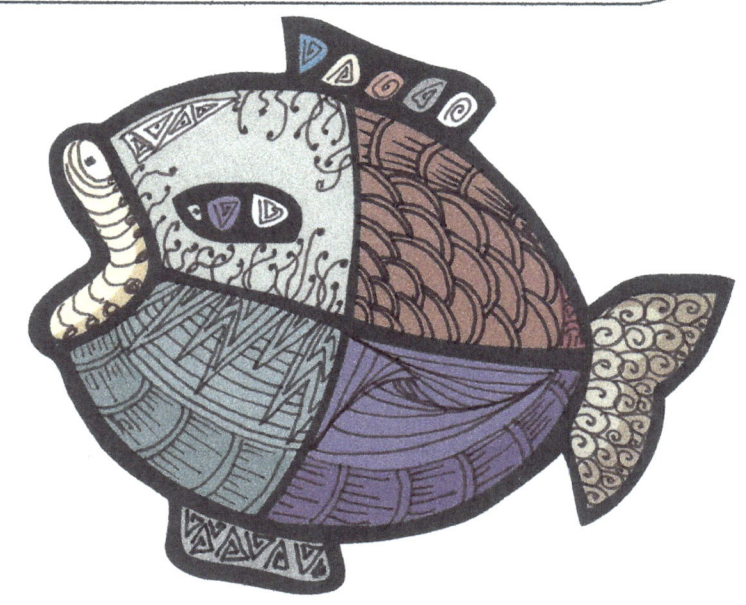

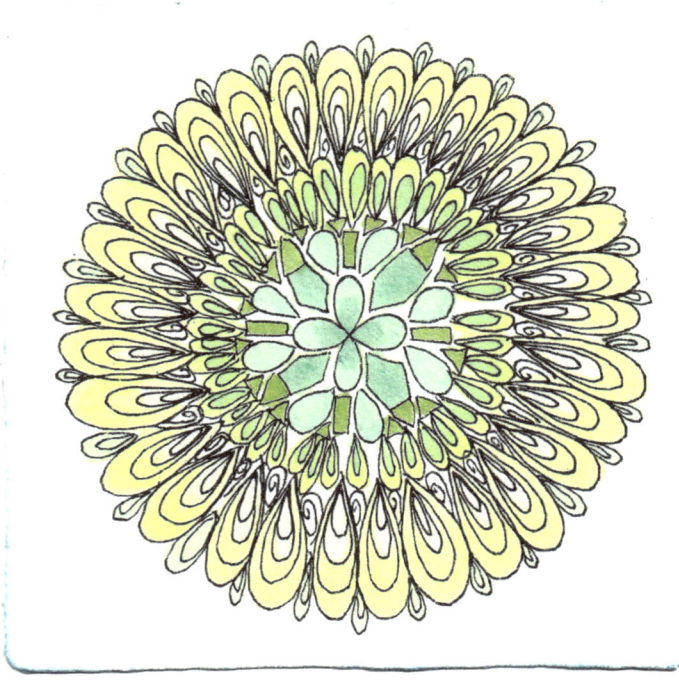

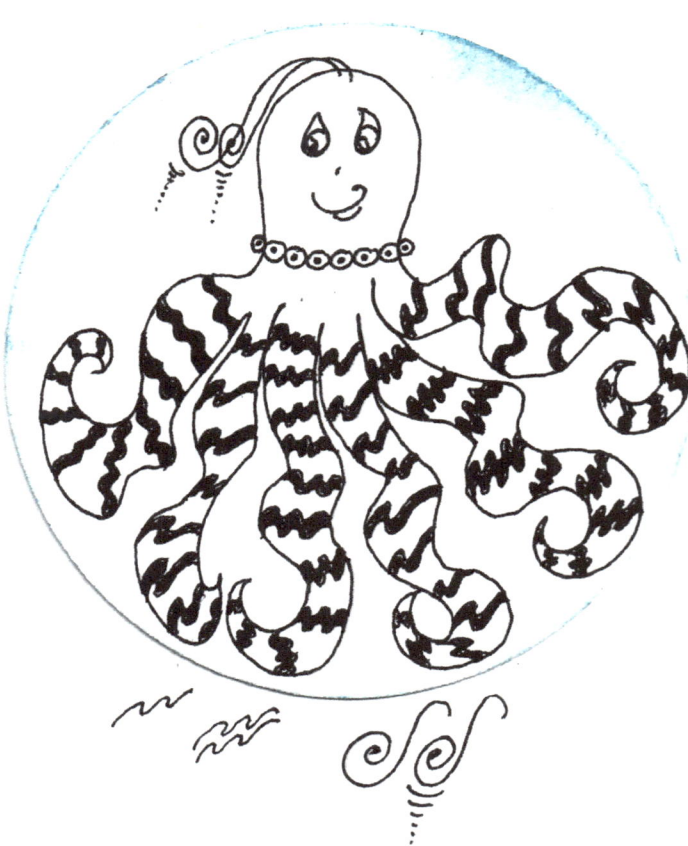

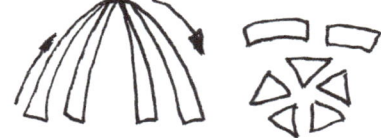

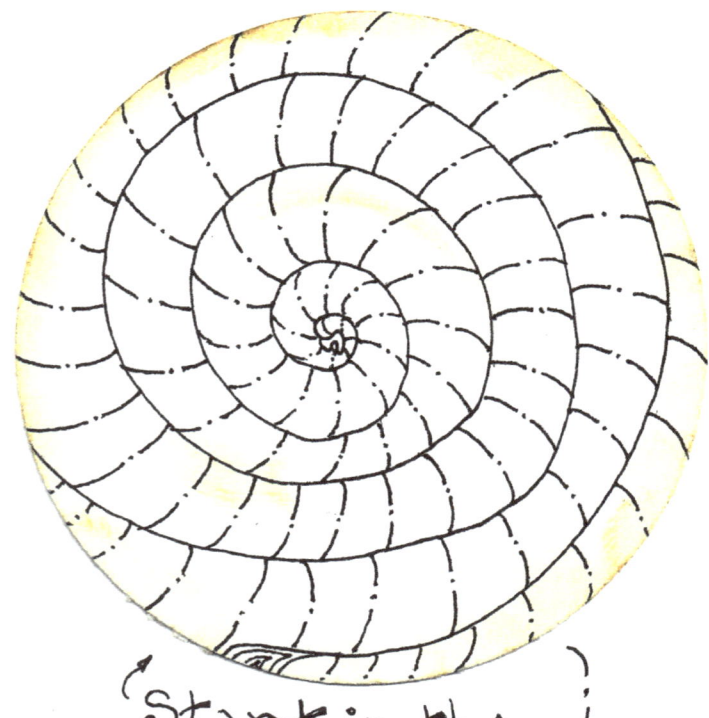

Start in the center

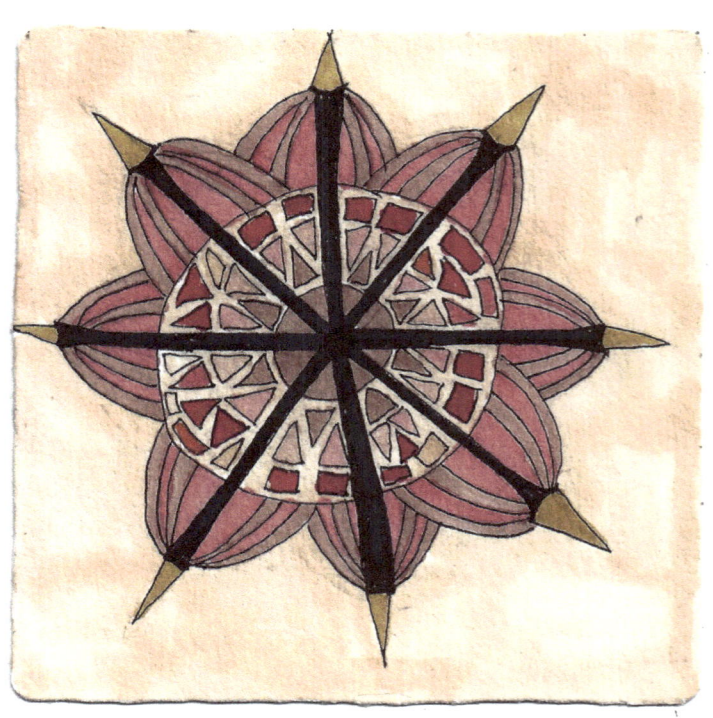

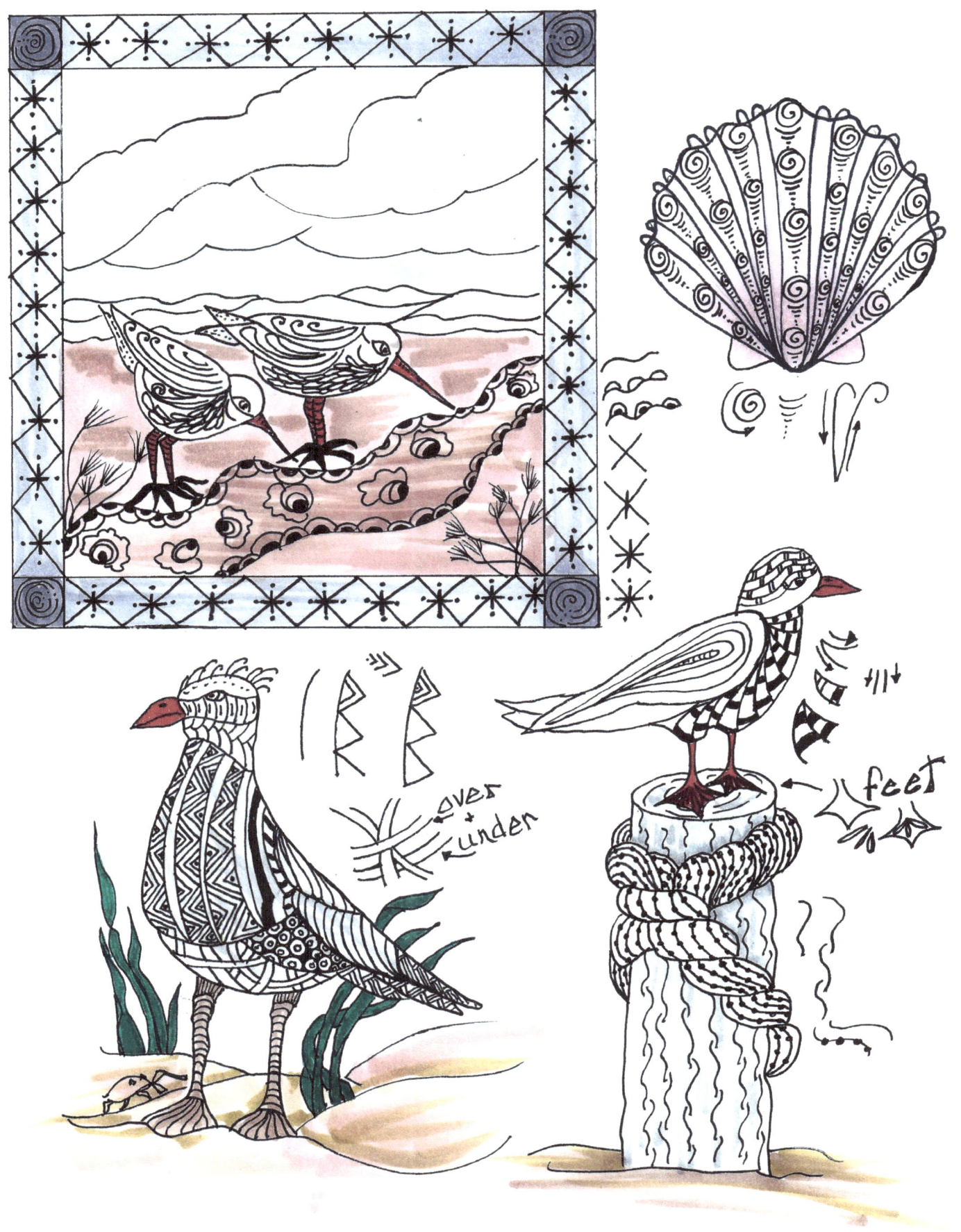

over + under

feet

The Beach

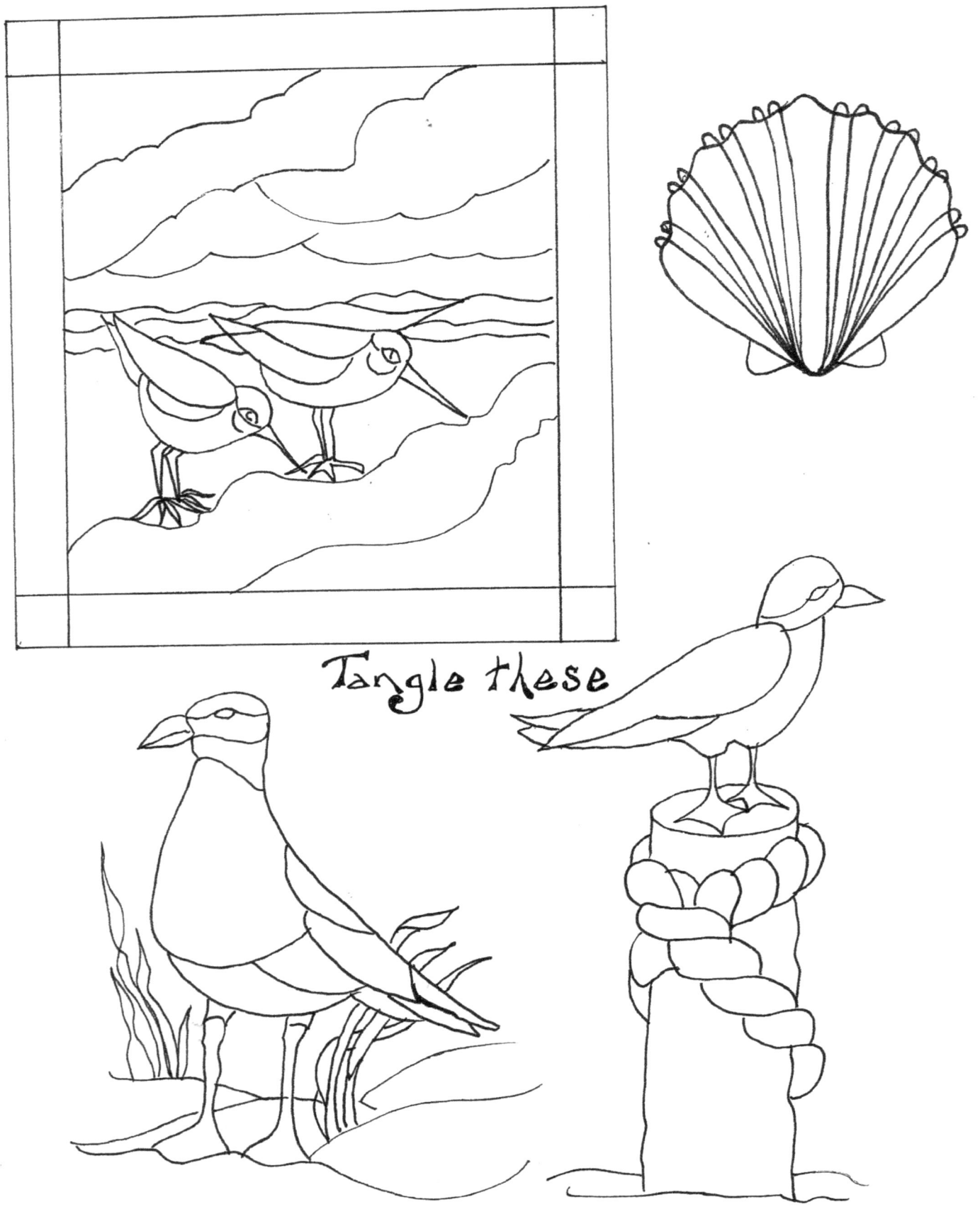

Tangle these

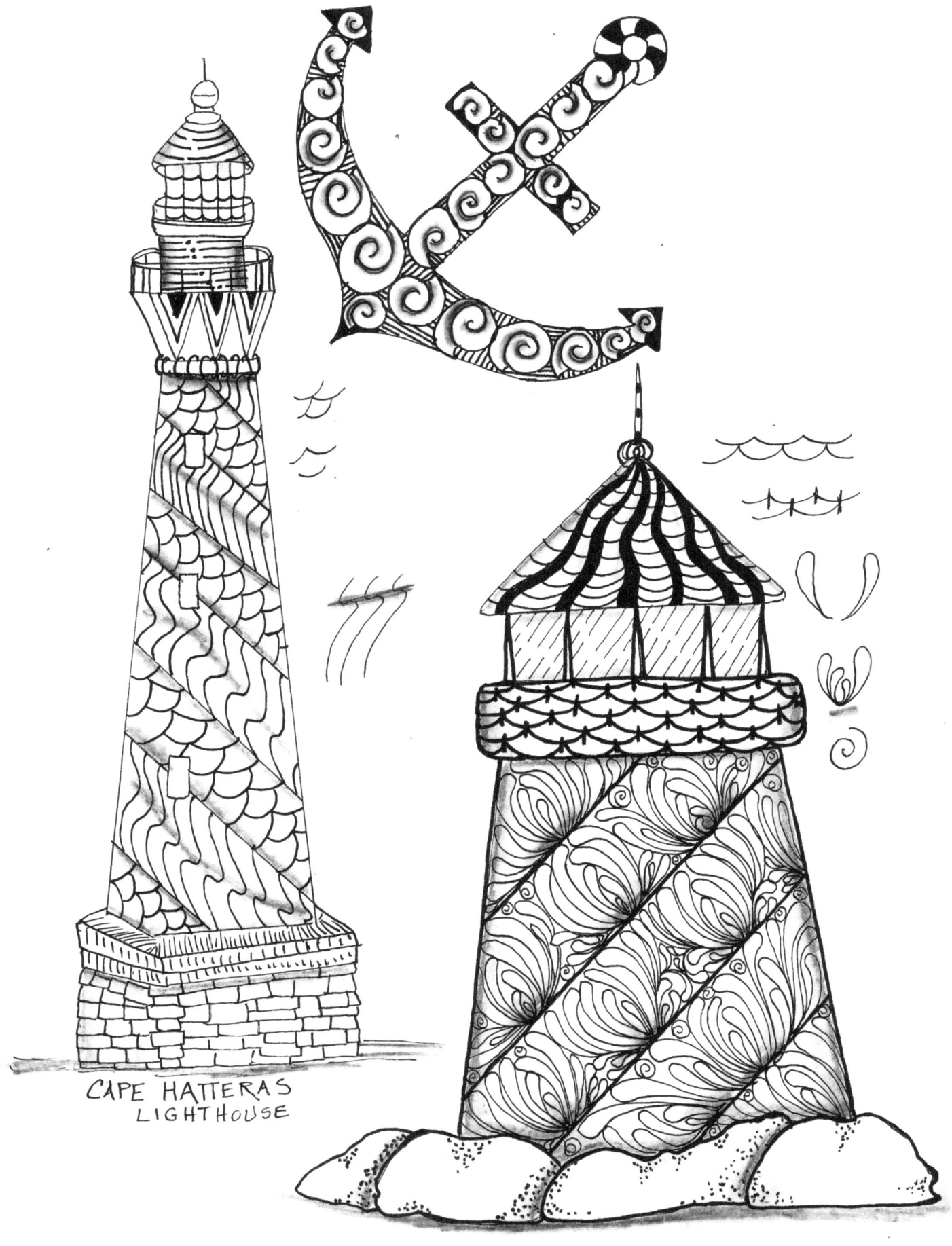

CAPE HATTERAS
LIGHTHOUSE

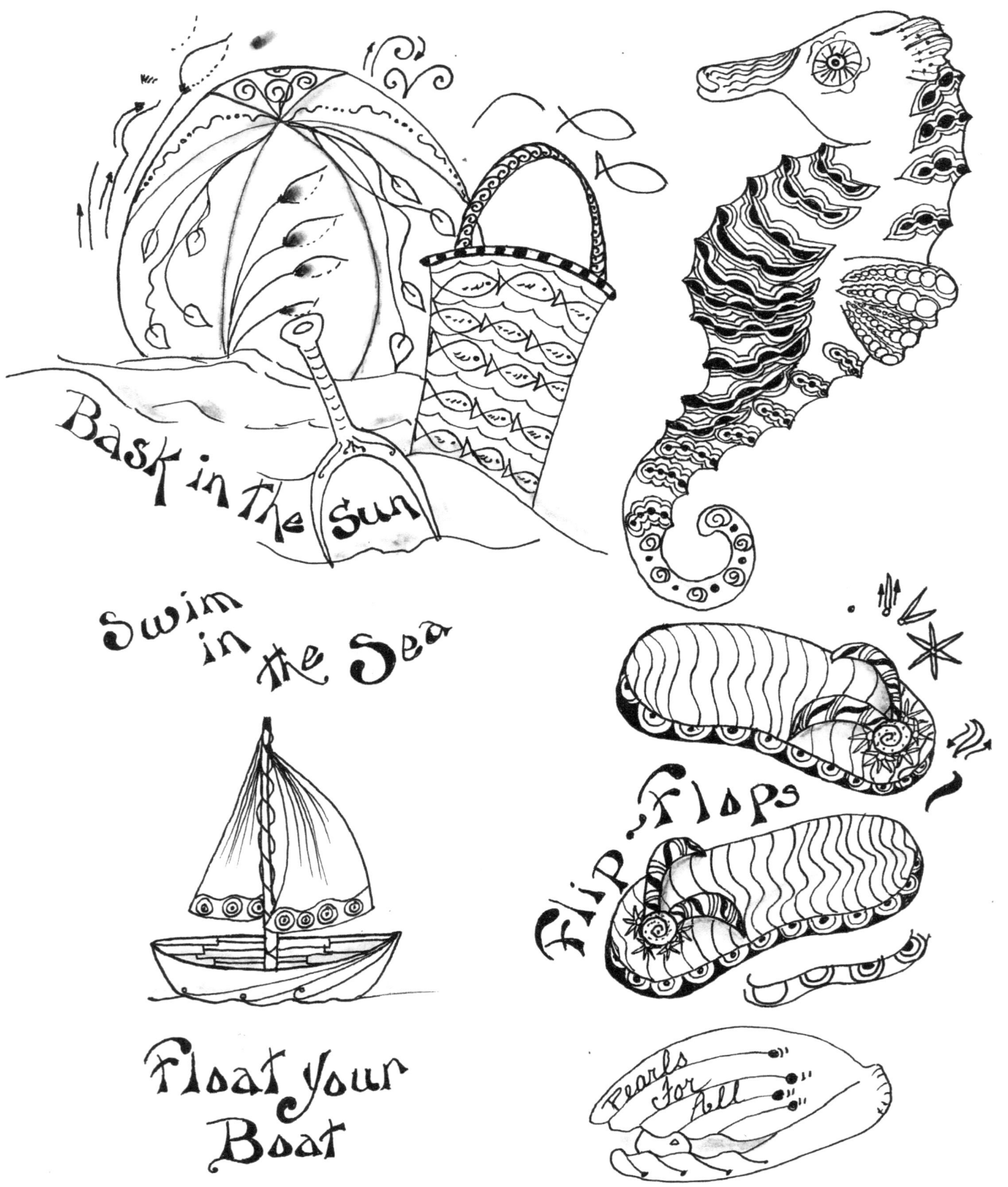

Bask in the Sun

Swim in the Sea

Float your Boat

Flip Flops

Pearls for All

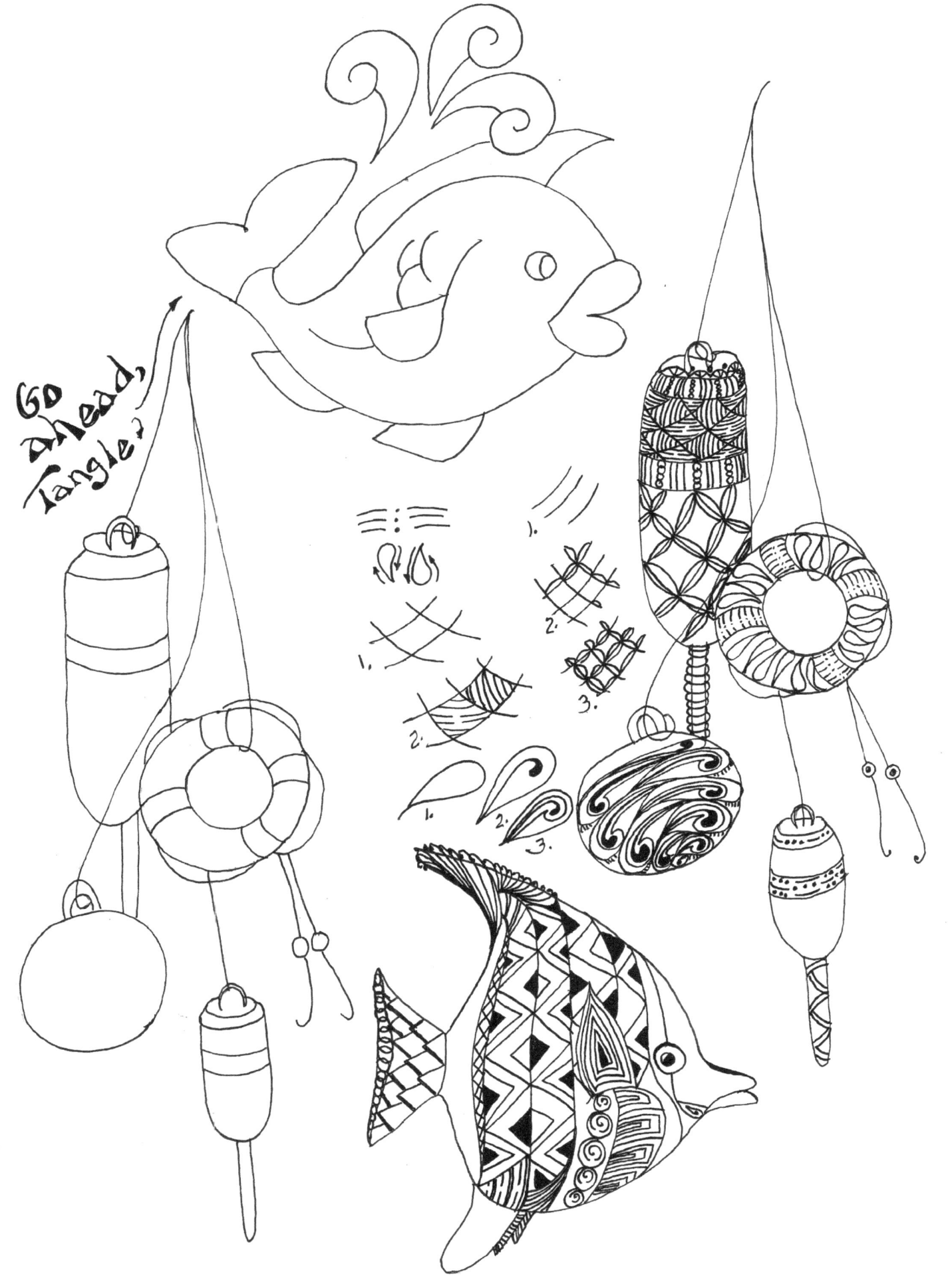

Go ahead, Tangle!

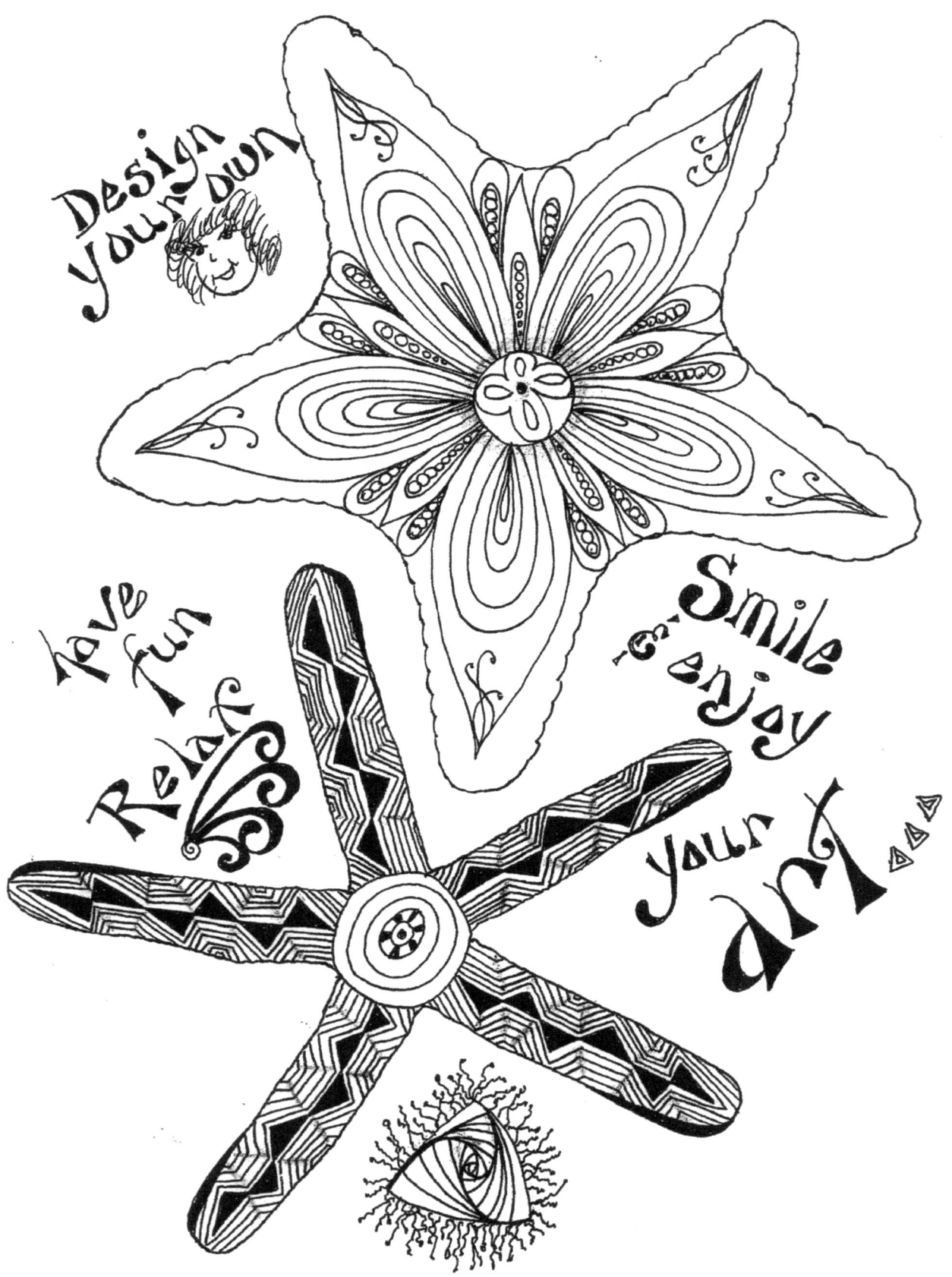

Design your own

Have fun Relax

Smile & enjoy your art...

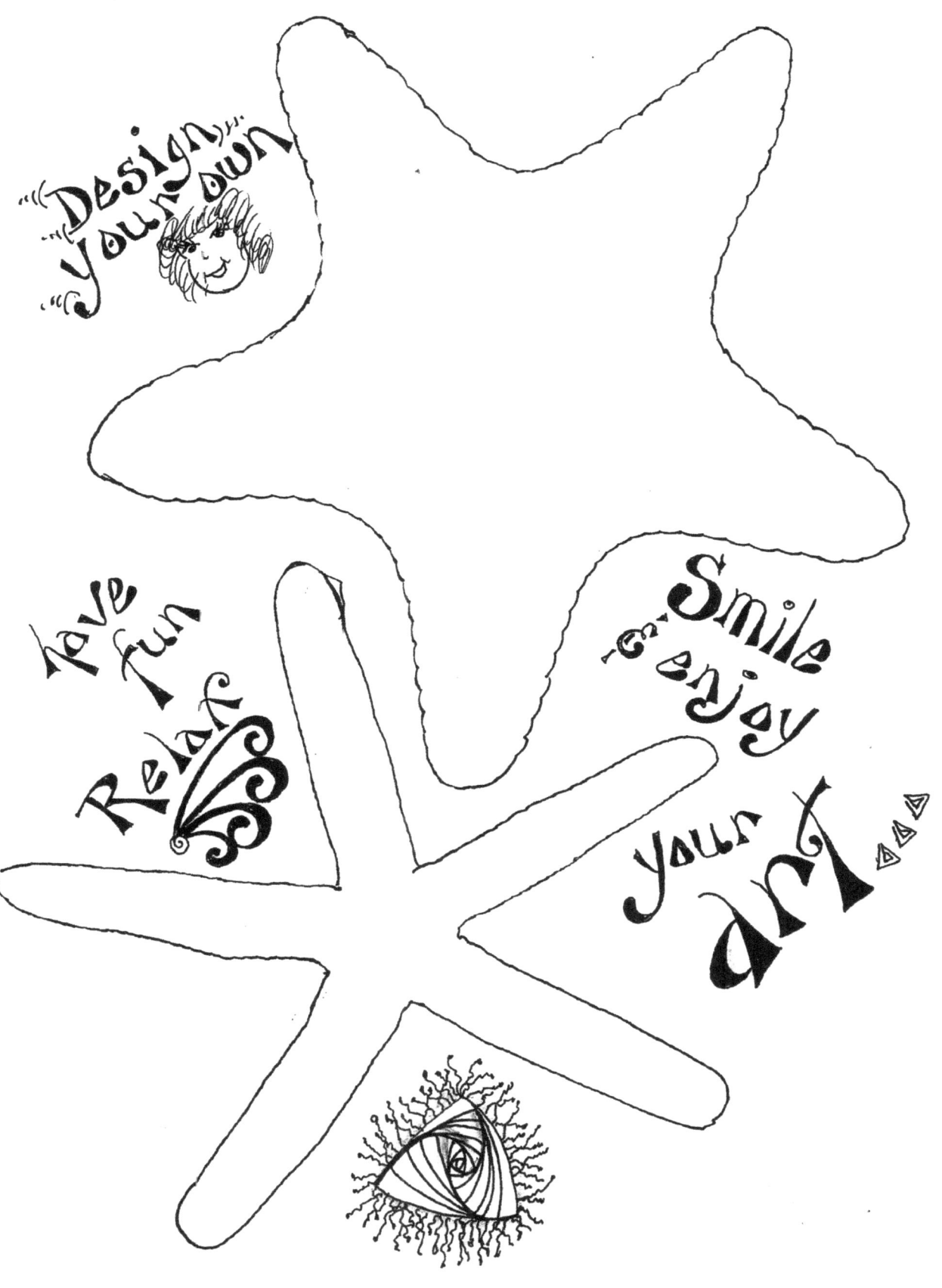

"Design" "your own"

have fun Relax

Smile & enjoy your art

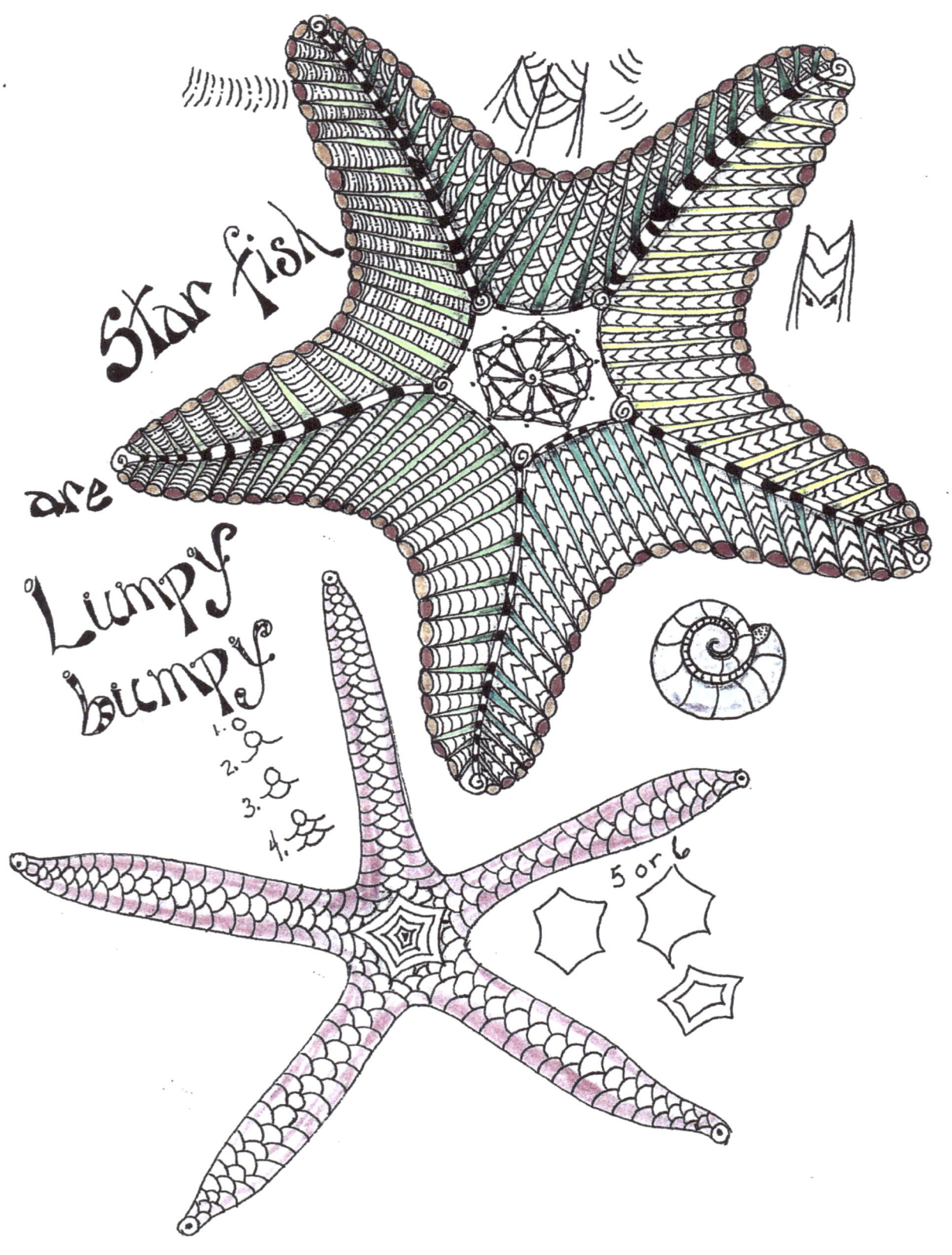

Star fish

are

Lumpy

bumpy

1. 𝒶
2. 𝒶
3. 𝒶
4. 𝒶

5 or 6

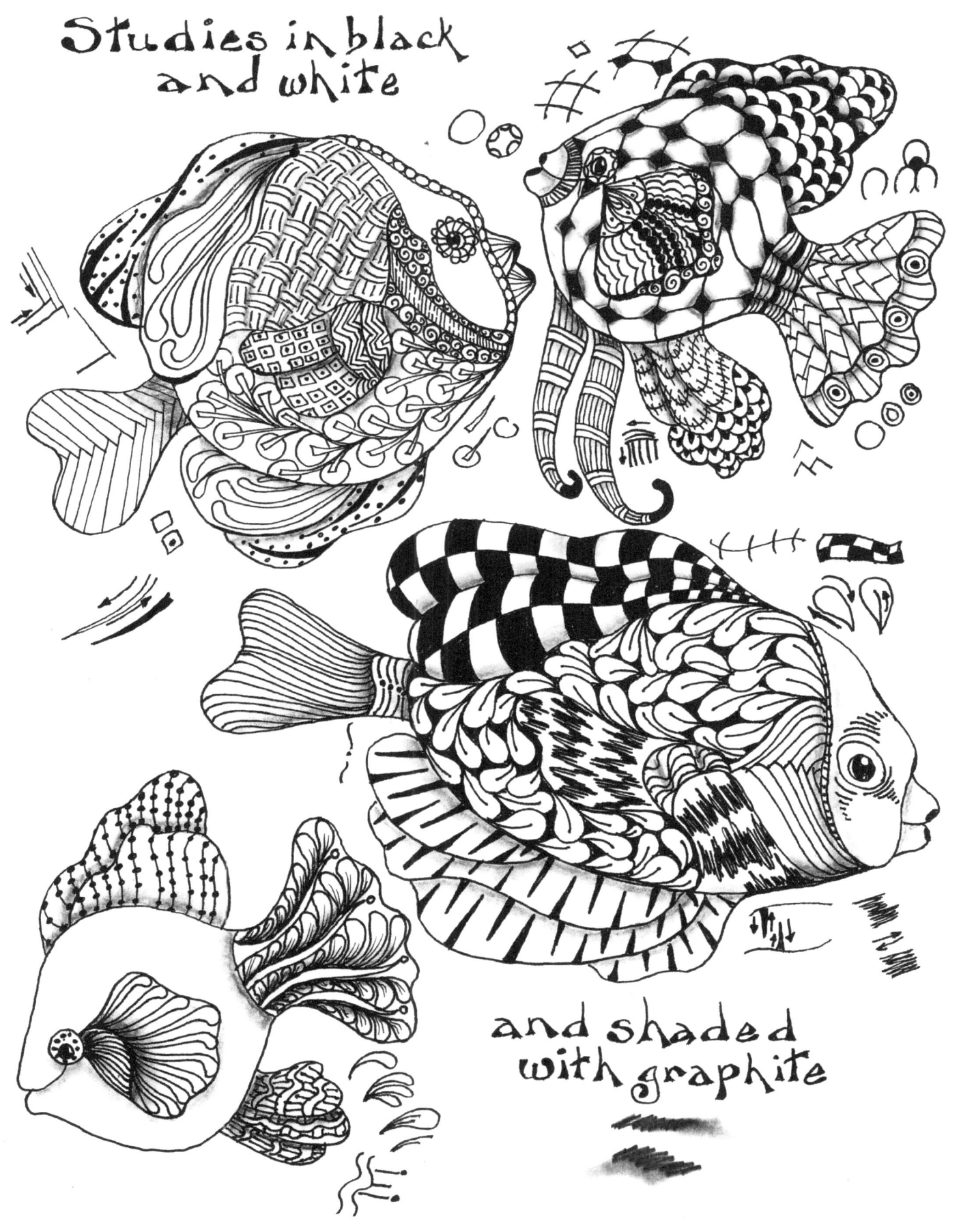

Studies in black
and white

and shaded
with graphite

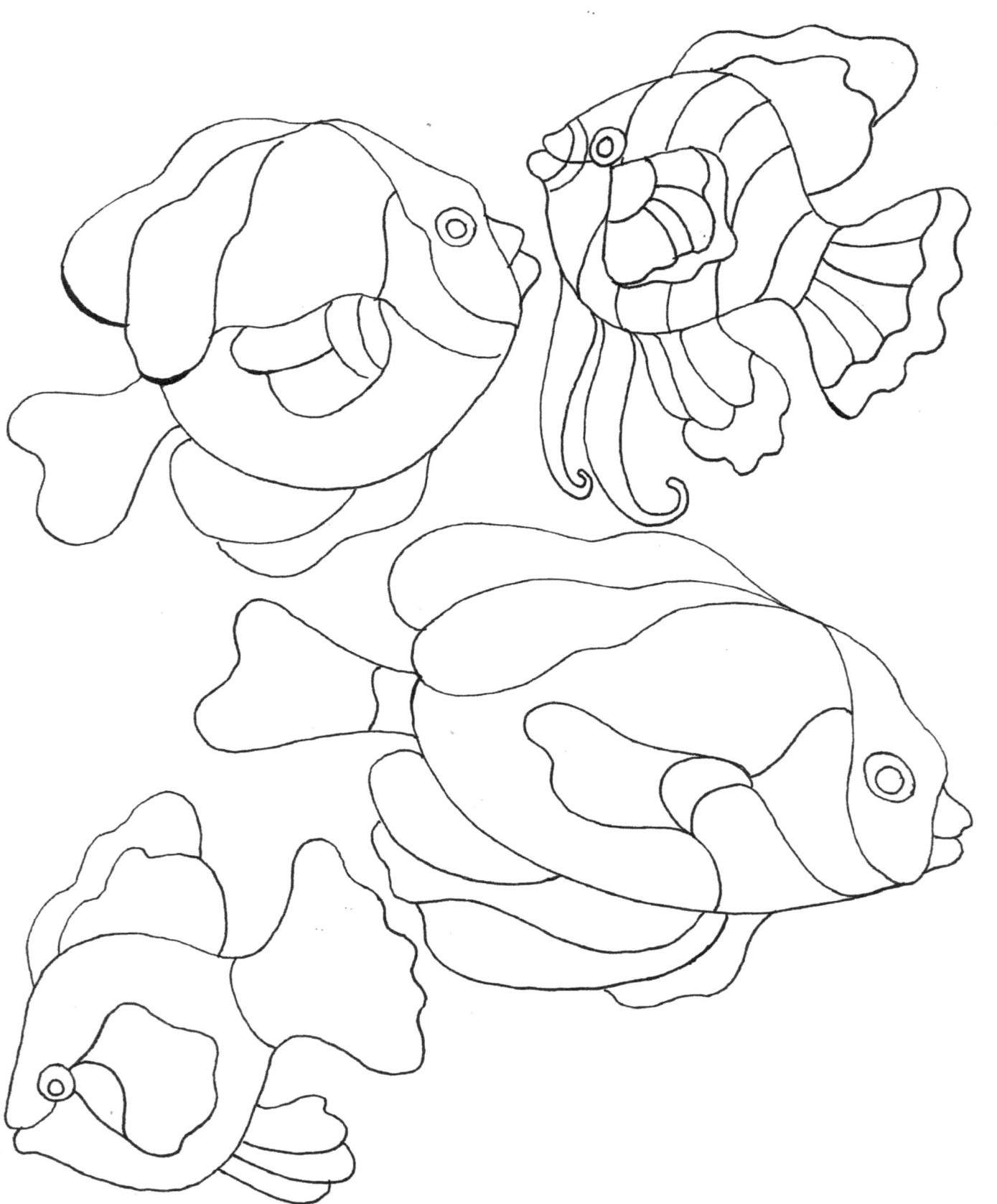

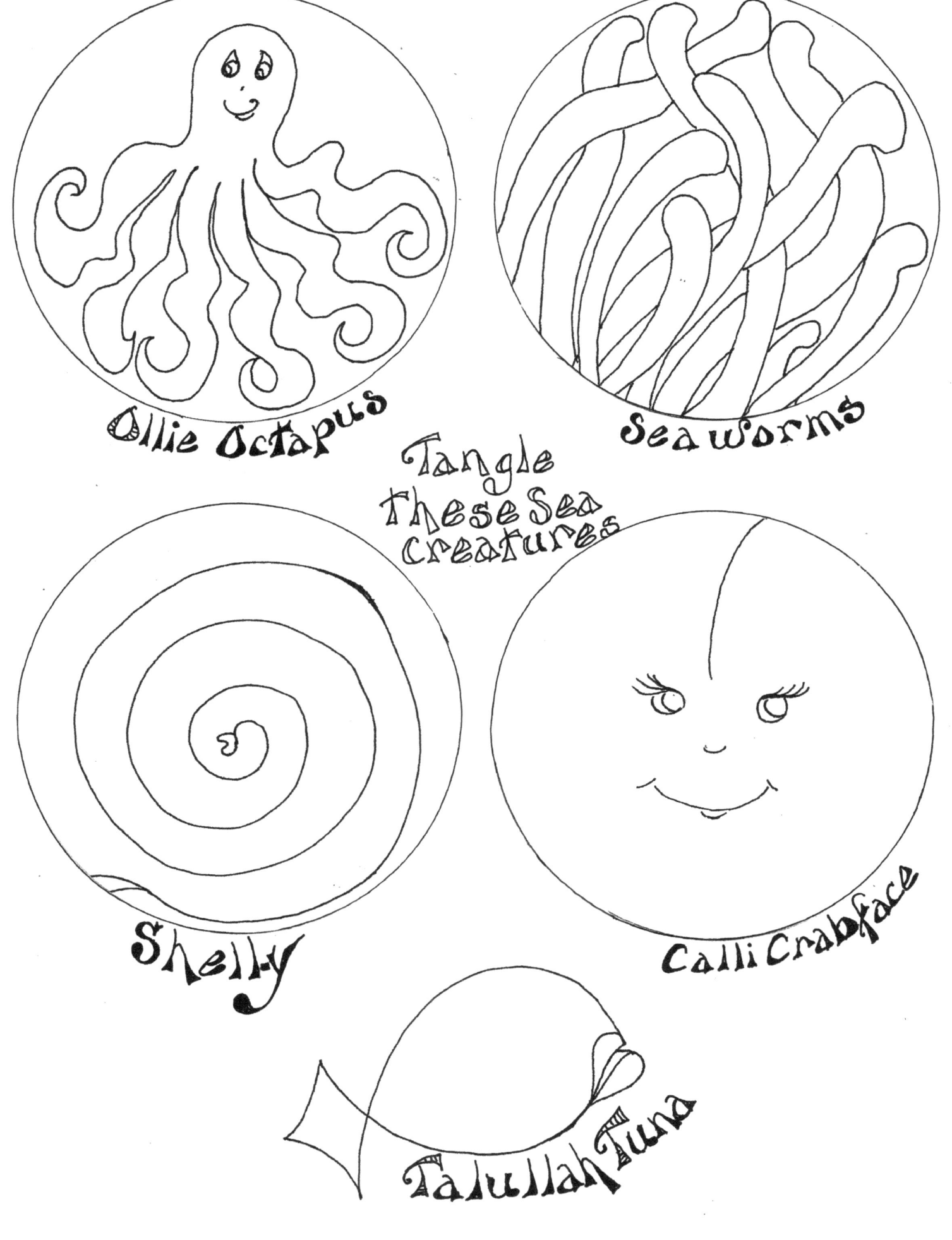

Ollie Octapus

Sea worms

Tangle
These Sea
Creatures

Shelly

Calli Crabface

Talullah Tuna

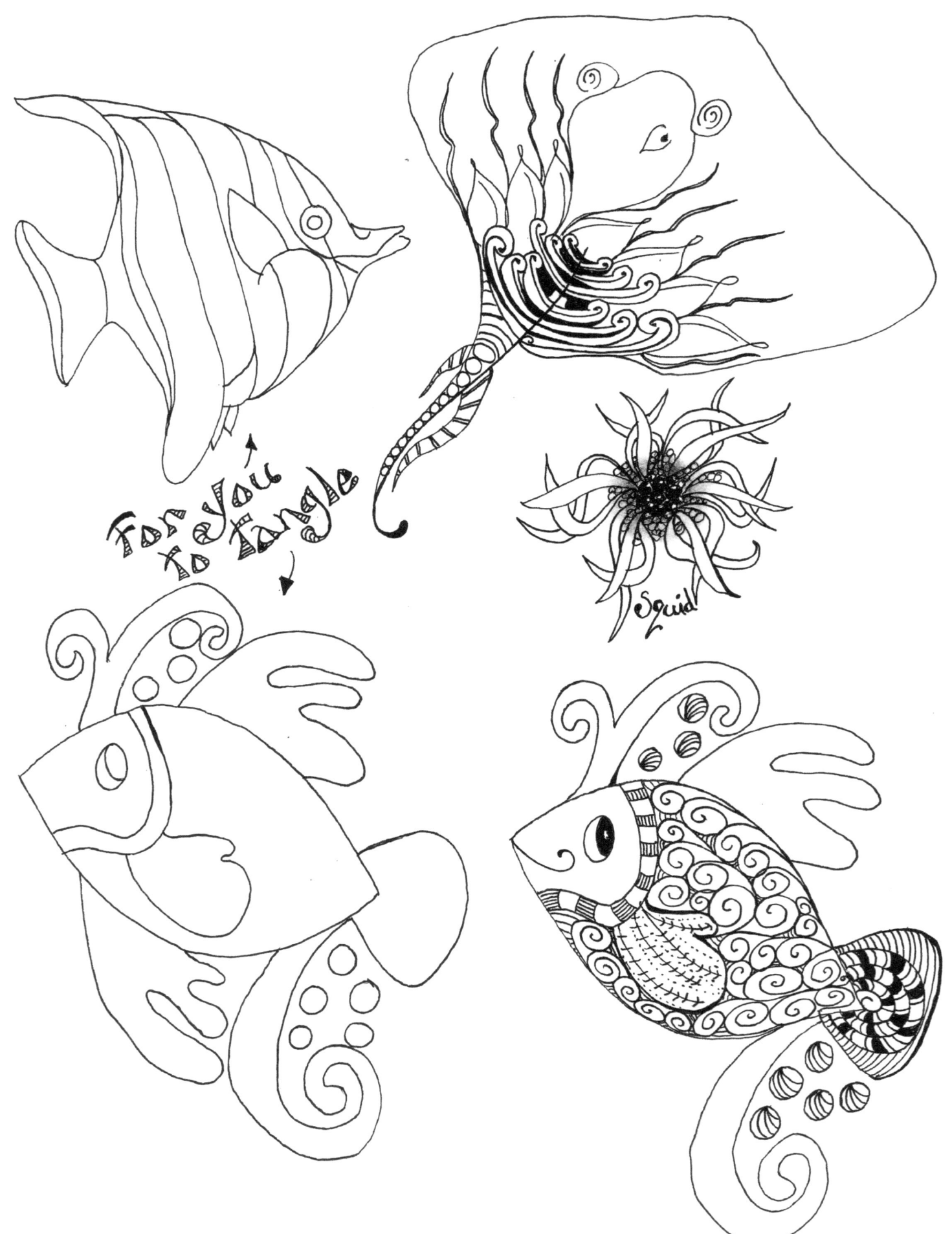

For you to Tangle

Squid

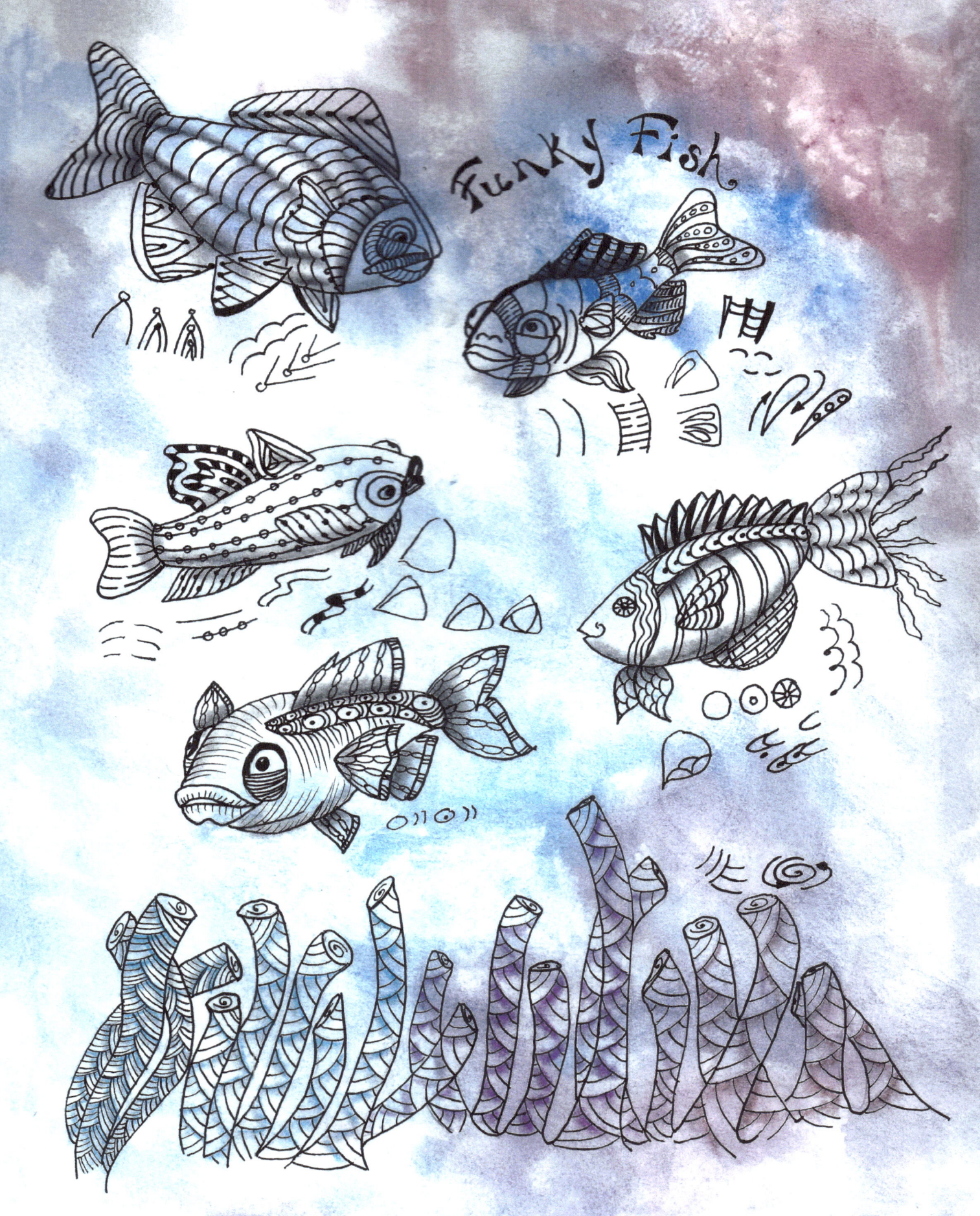

Funky Fish

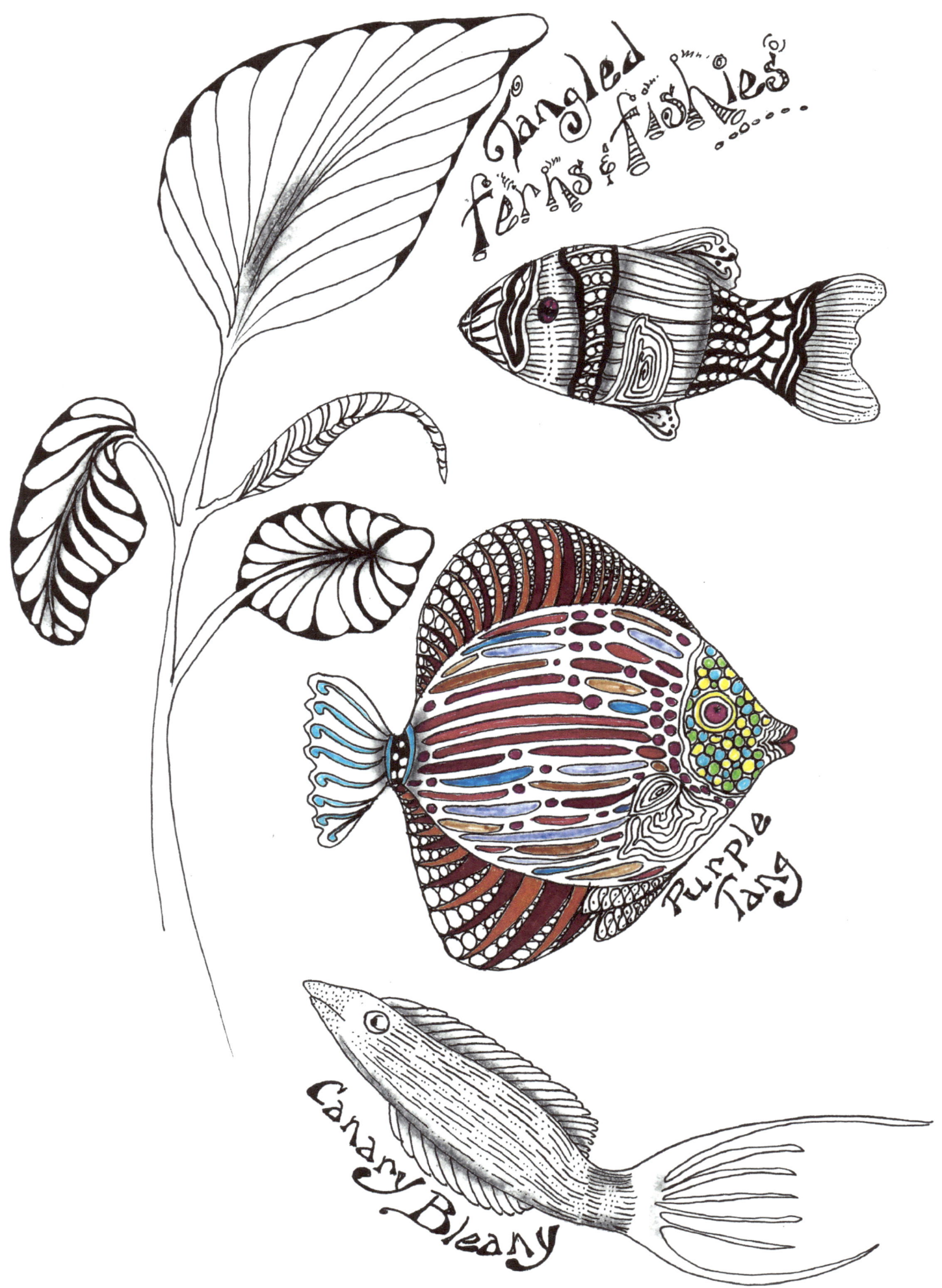

Tangled Ferns & Fishies......

Purple Tang

Canary Bleany

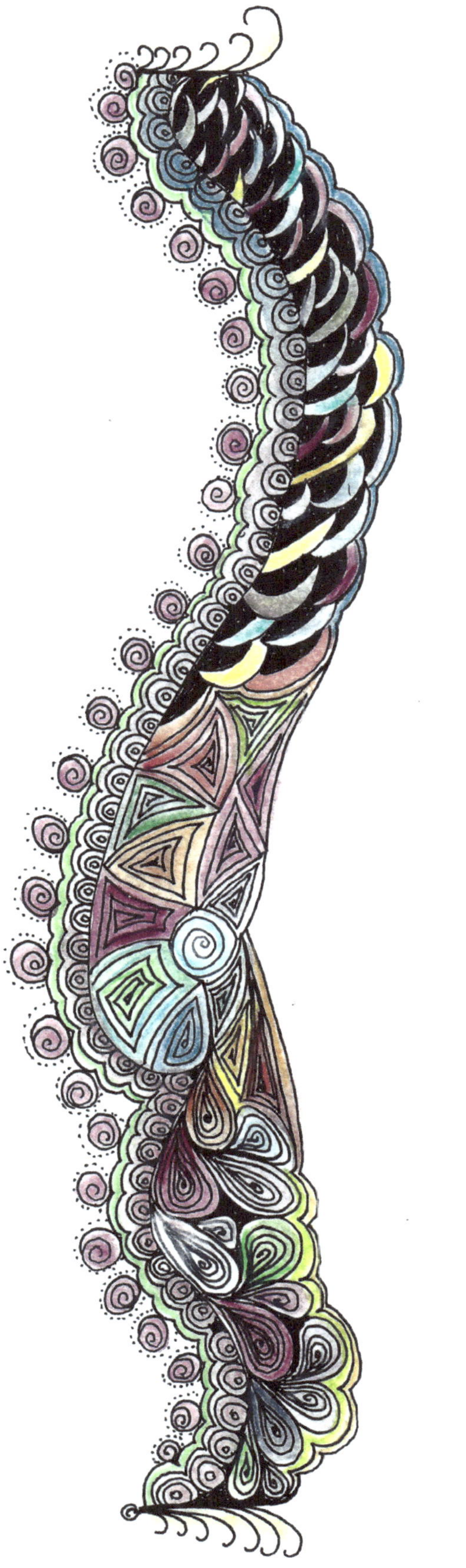

PYGMY
CHAIN SWORD
PLANT →

Goosebumps

Have
fun

Sea Snail
(My style)

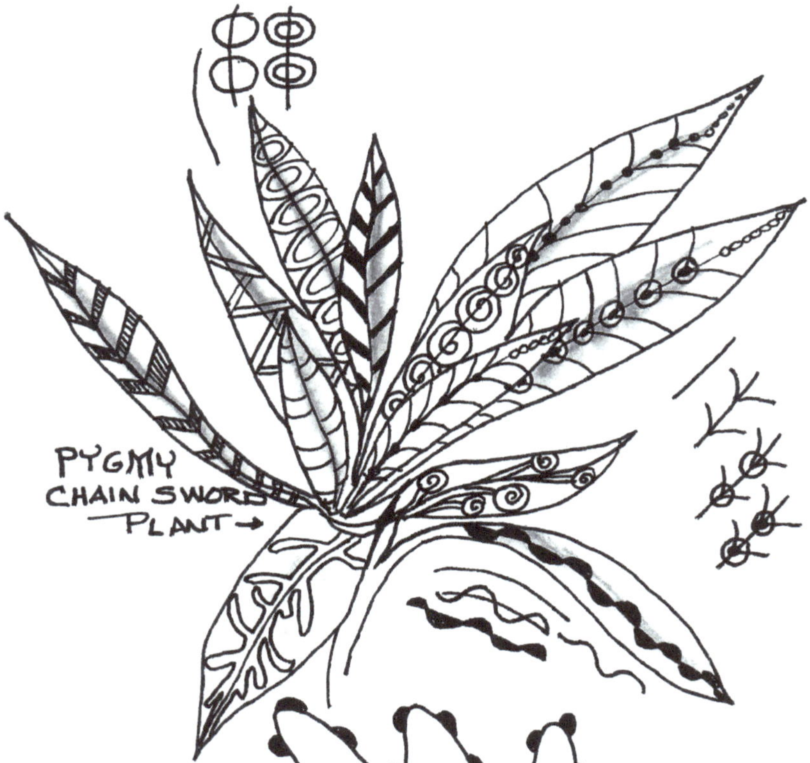

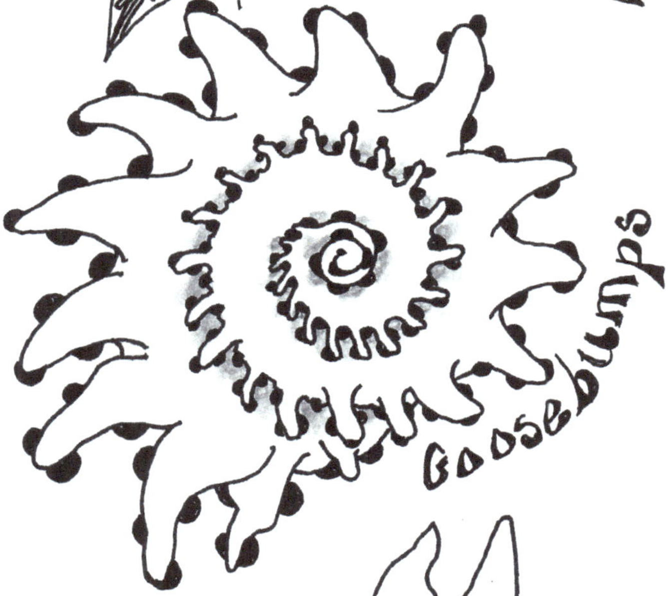

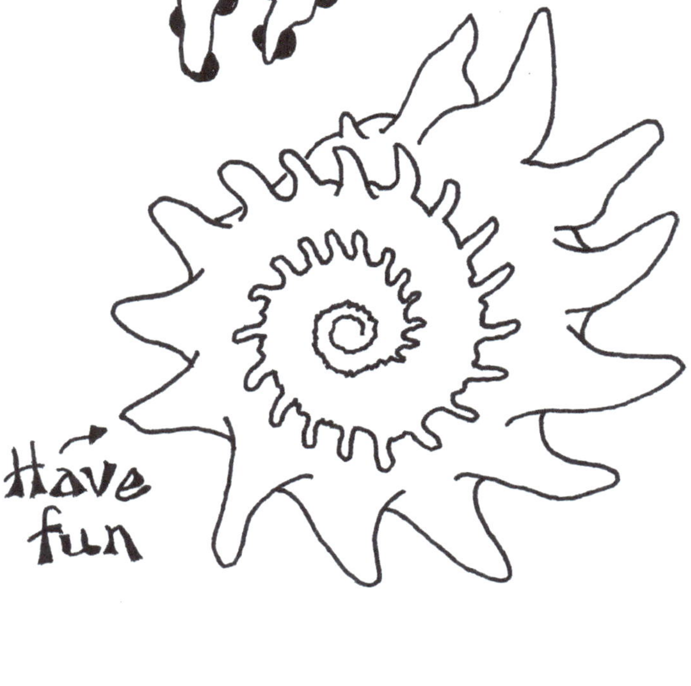

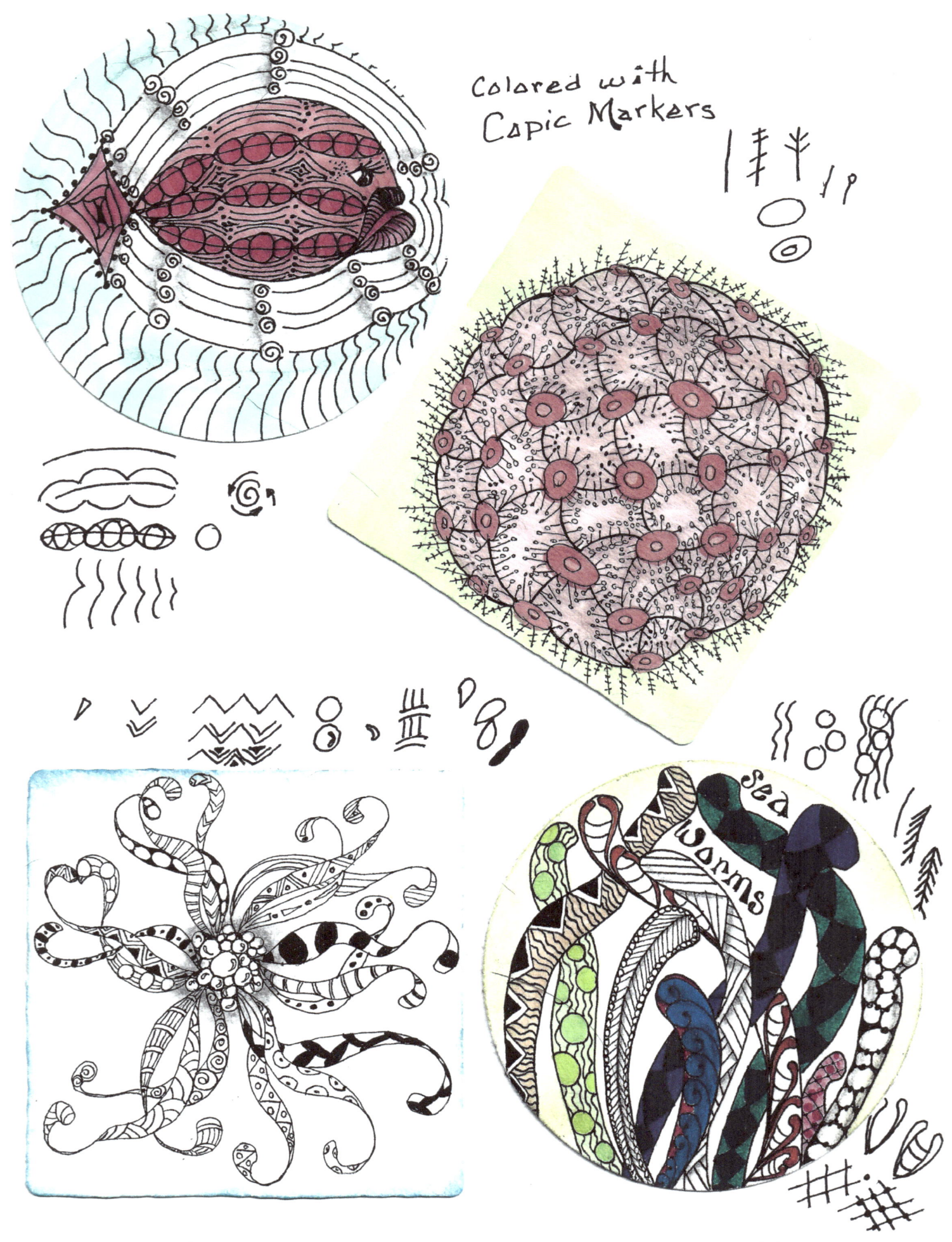

Colored with
Capic Markers

Sea
Worms

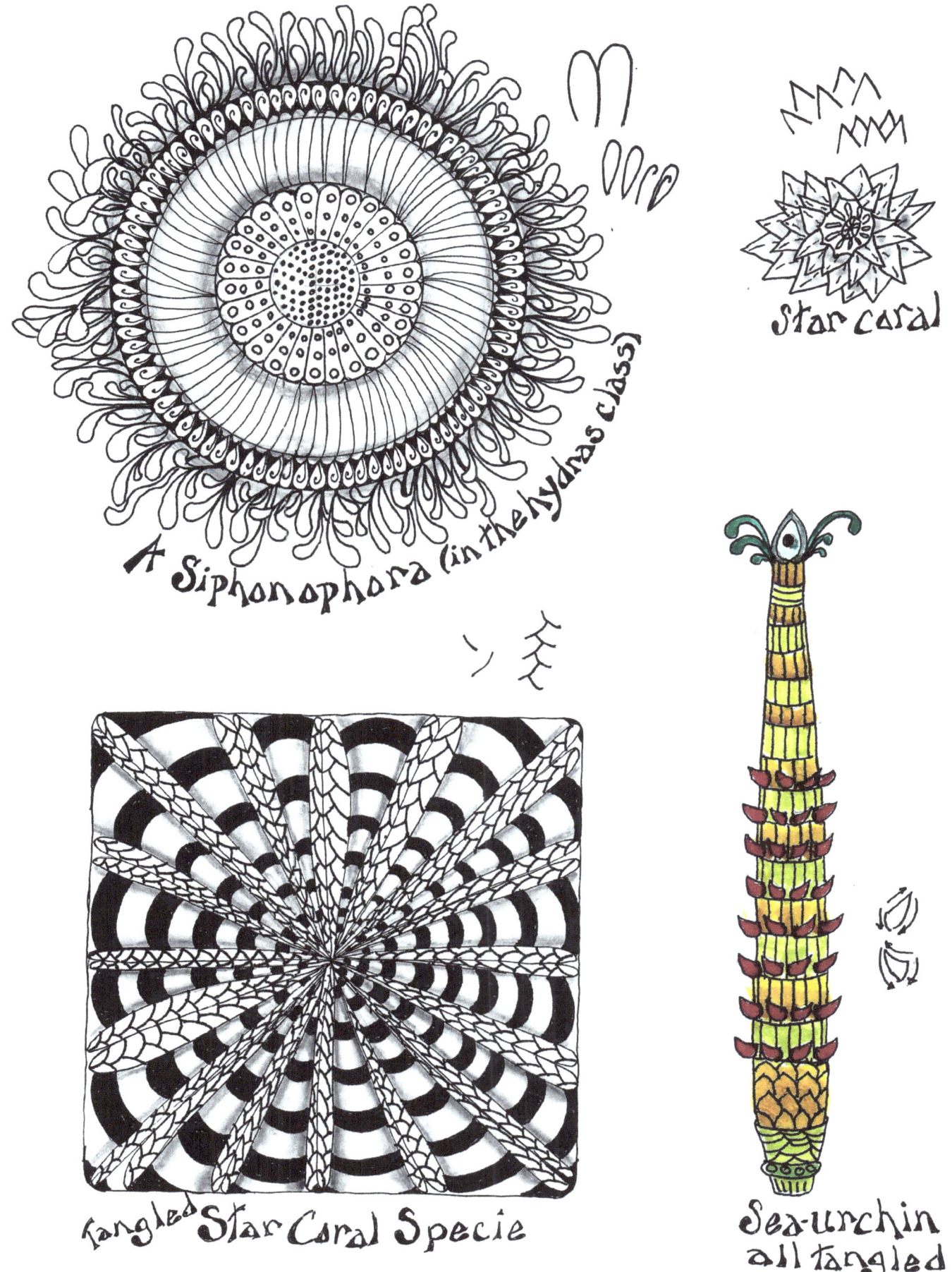

A Siphonophora (in the hydras class)

Star coral

tangled Star Coral Specie

Sea-urchin
all tangled

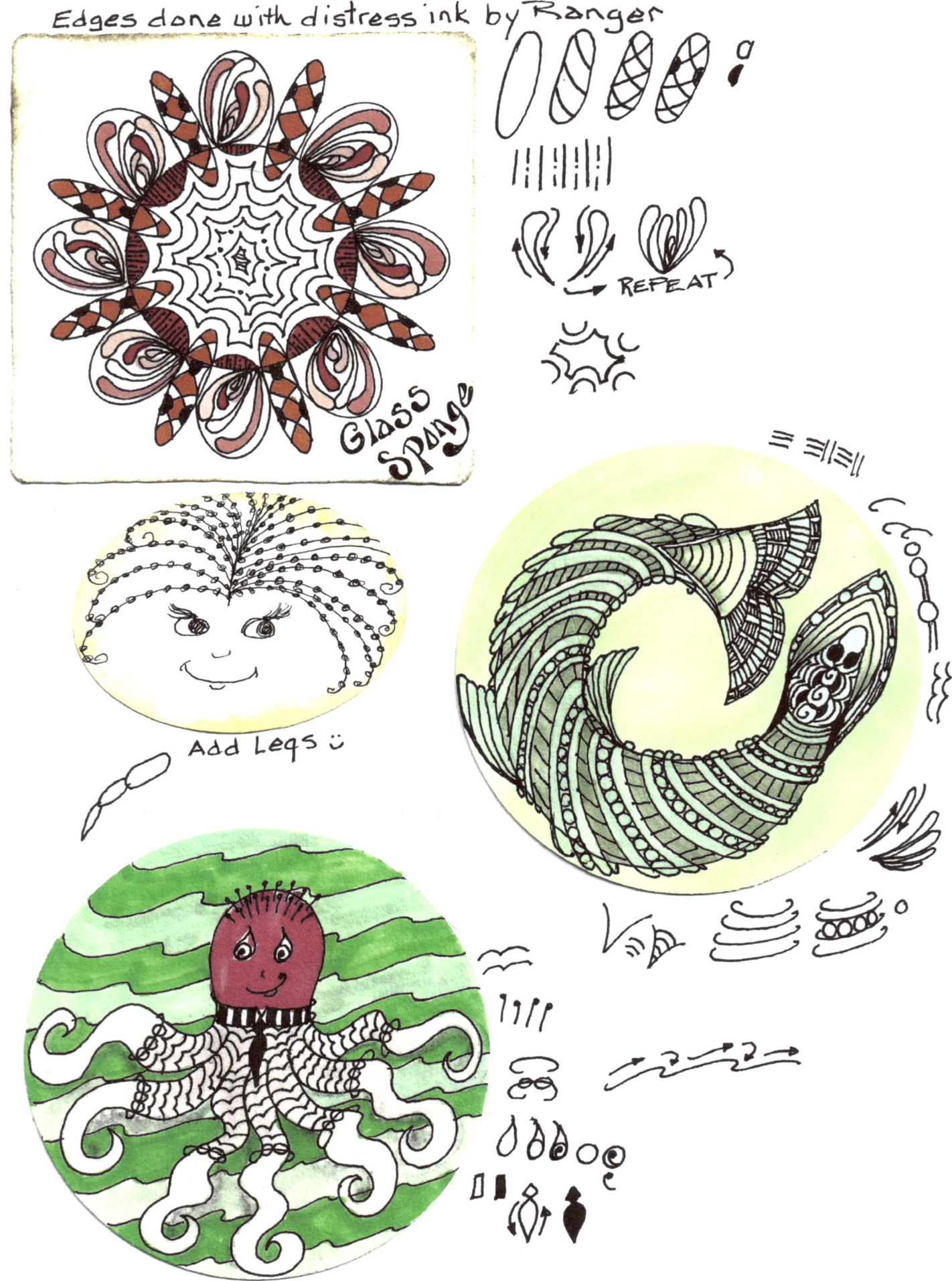

Edges done with distress ink by Ranger

Glass Sponge

Add Legs ☺

REPEAT

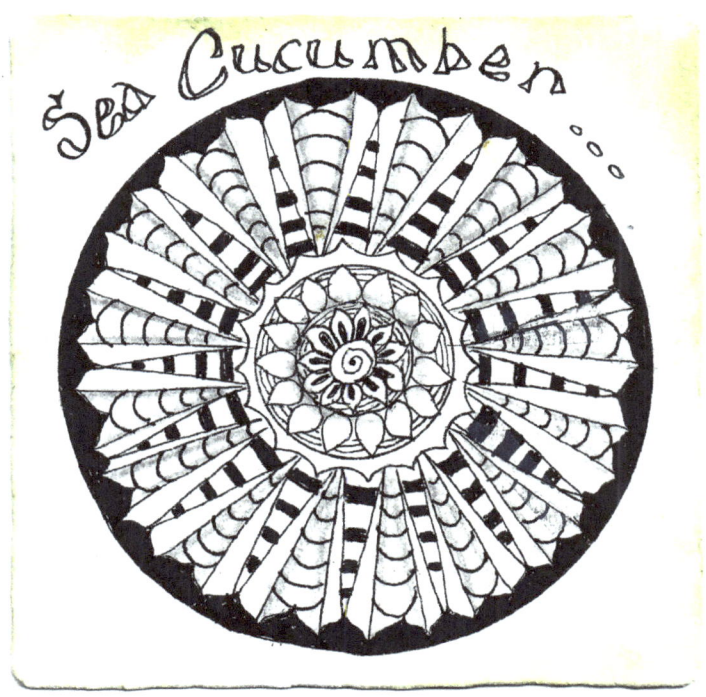

Sea Cucumber...

All edges are colored with Ranger® distress ink.

Circle border is black ink

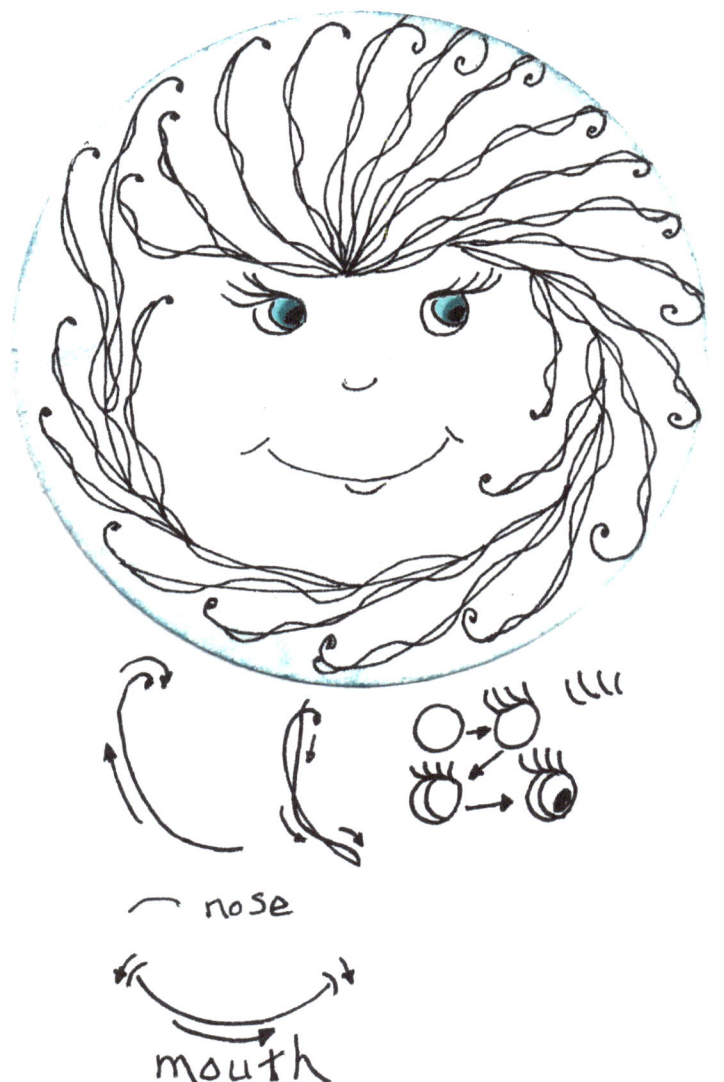

nose

mouth

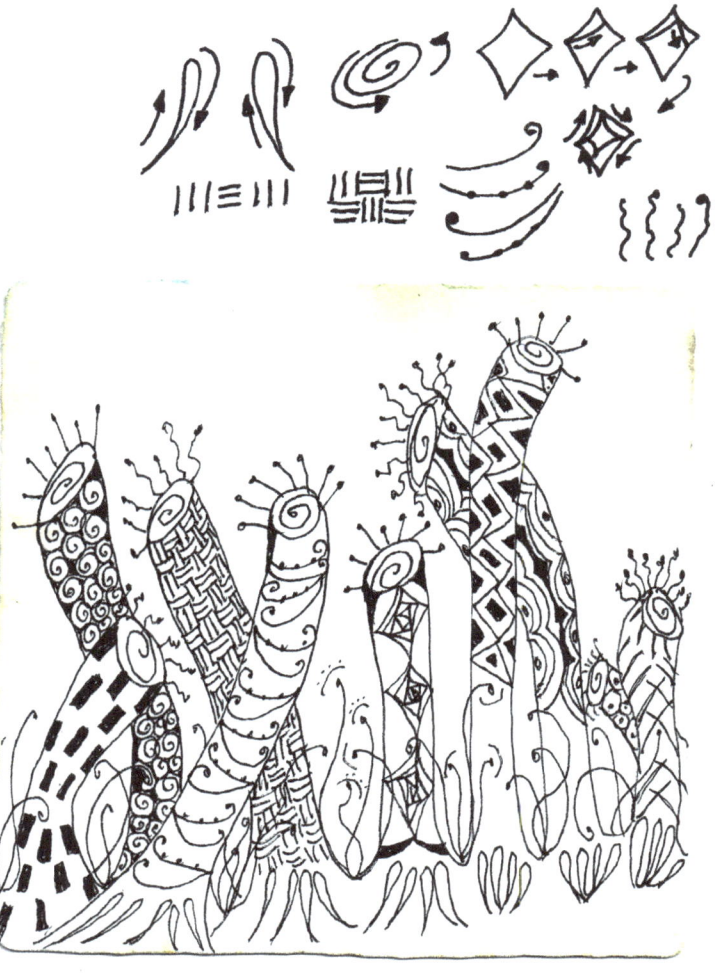

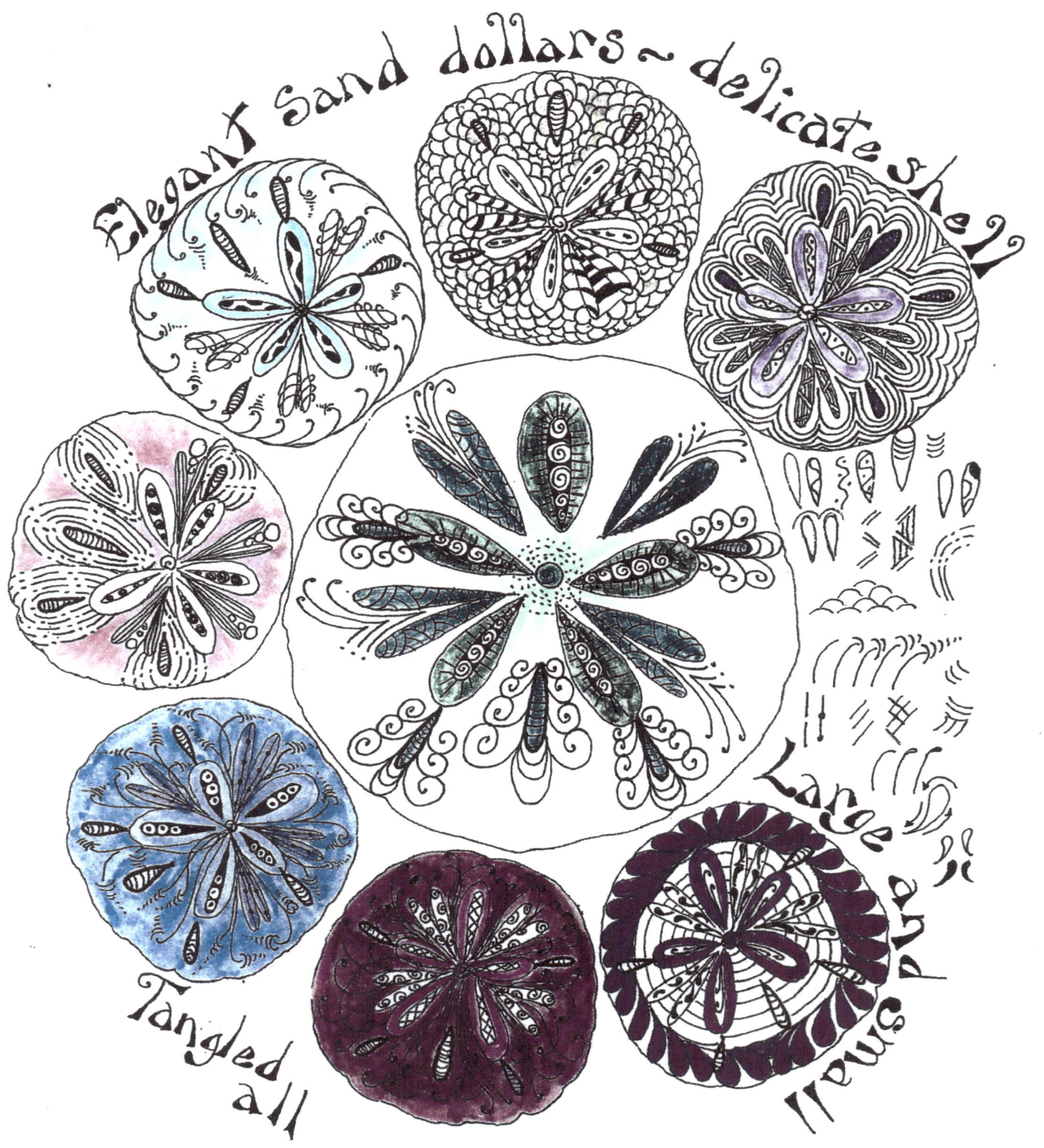

Elegant sand dollars ~ delicate shell

Large and small

Tangled all

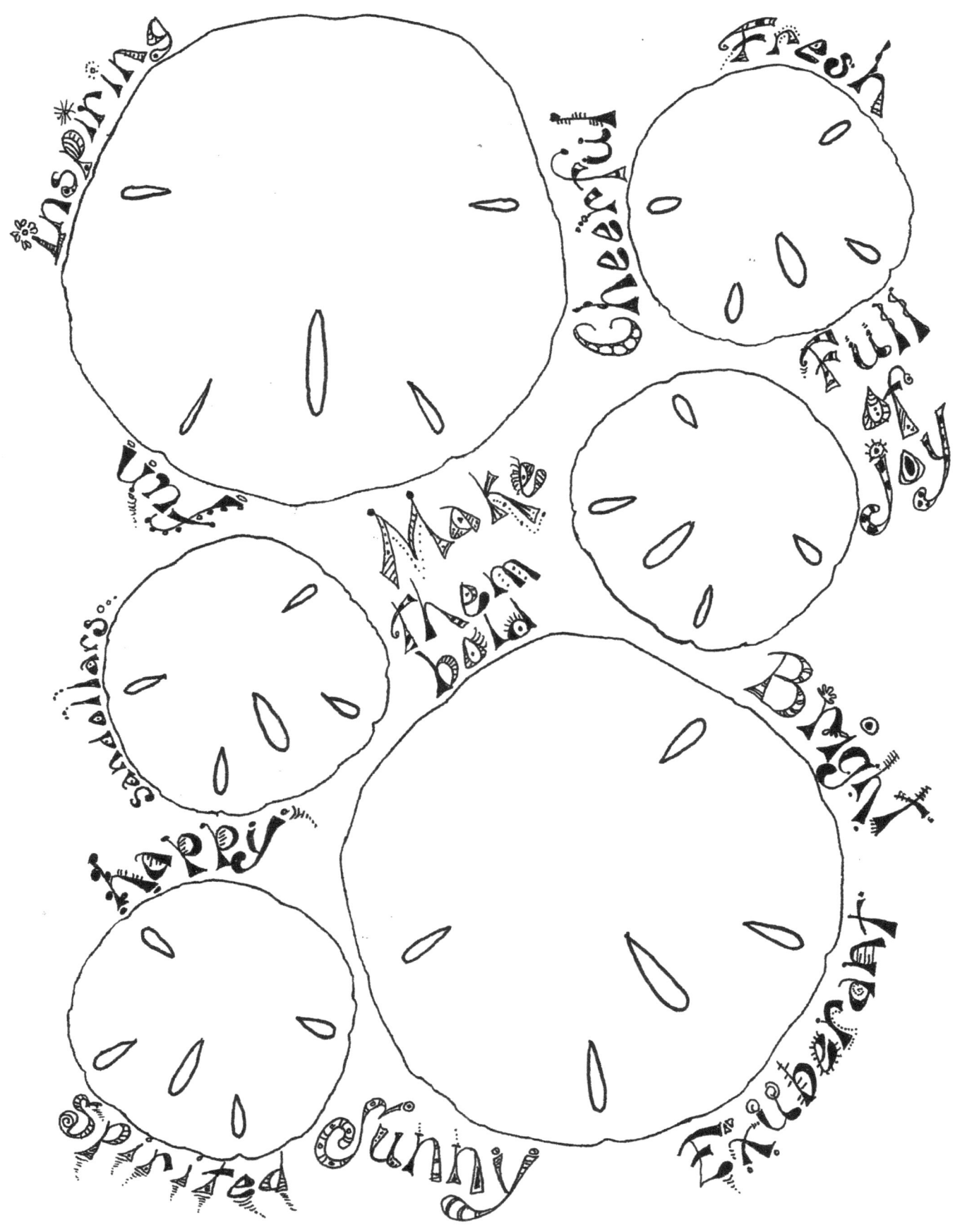

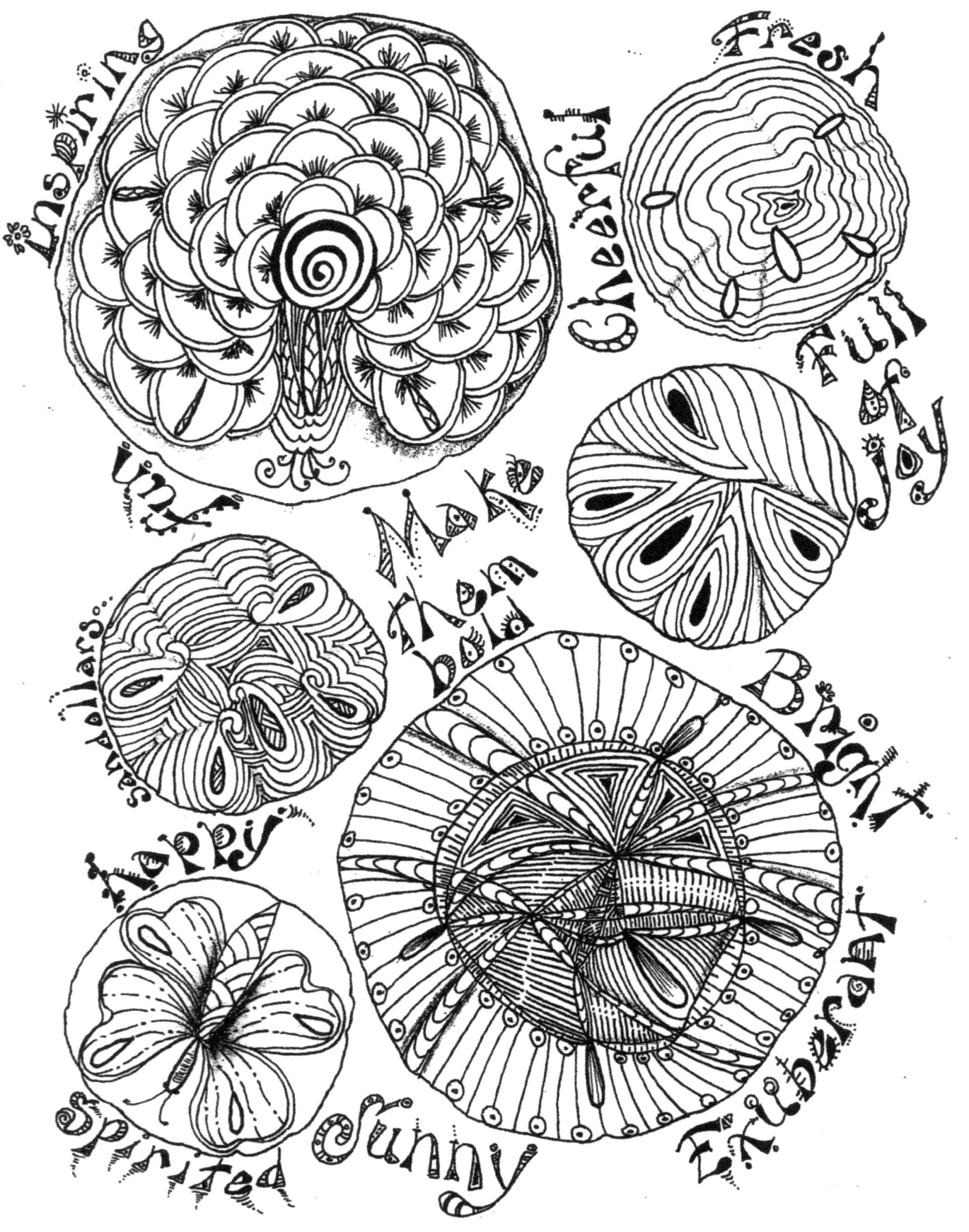

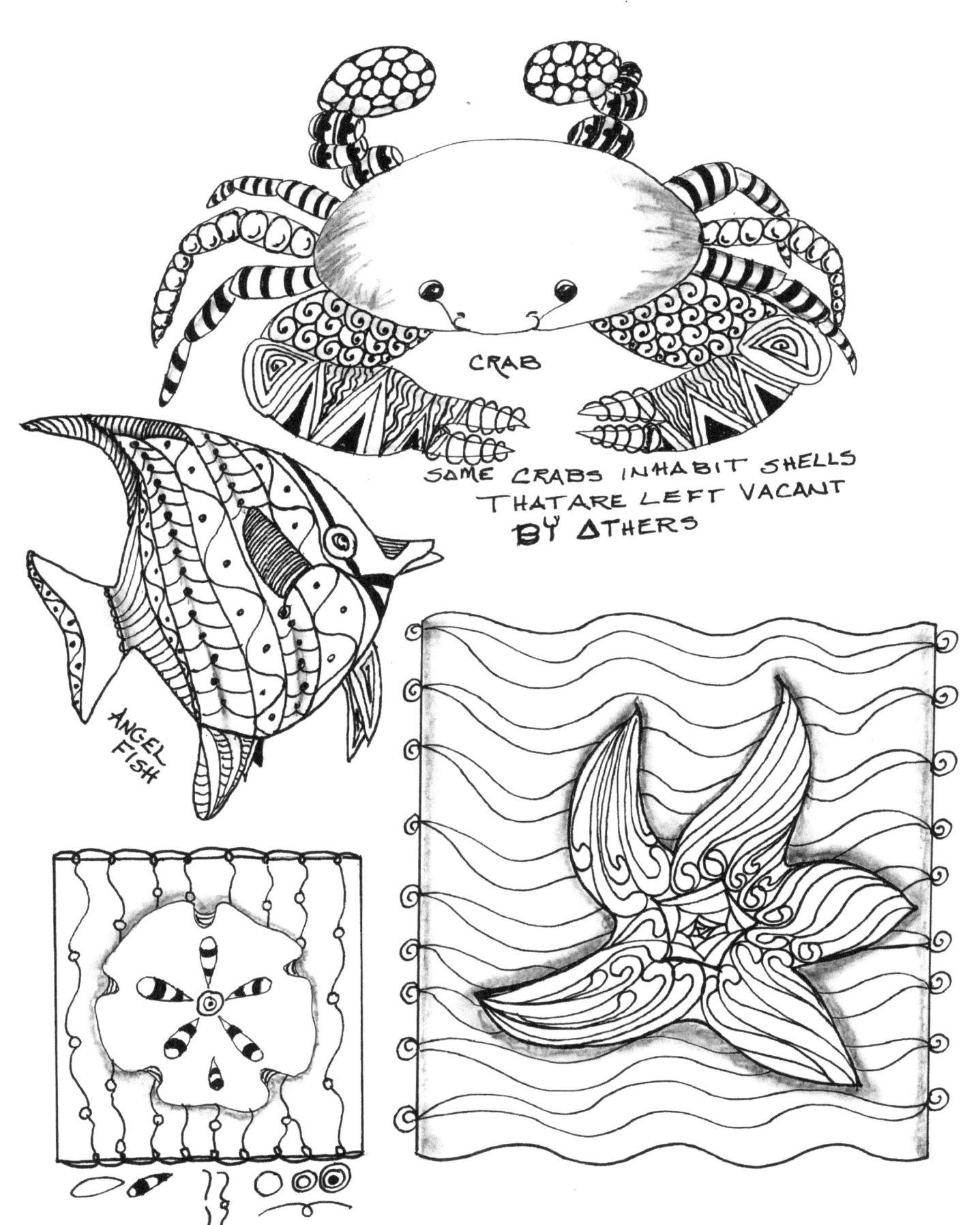

CRAB

SOME CRABS INHABIT SHELLS
THAT ARE LEFT VACANT
BY OTHERS

ANGEL
FISH

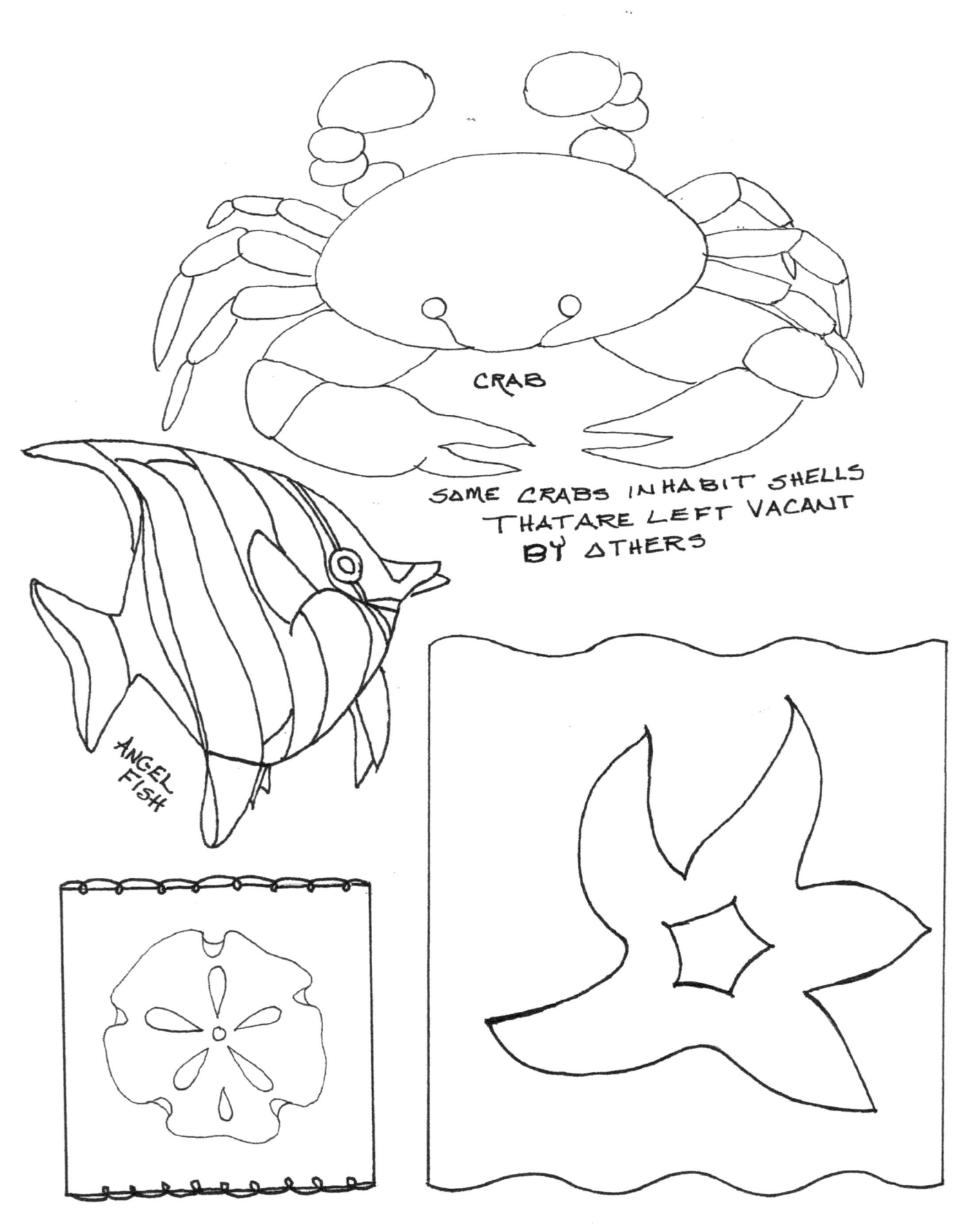

CRAB

SOME CRABS INHABIT SHELLS
THAT ARE LEFT VACANT
BY OTHERS

ANGEL
FISH

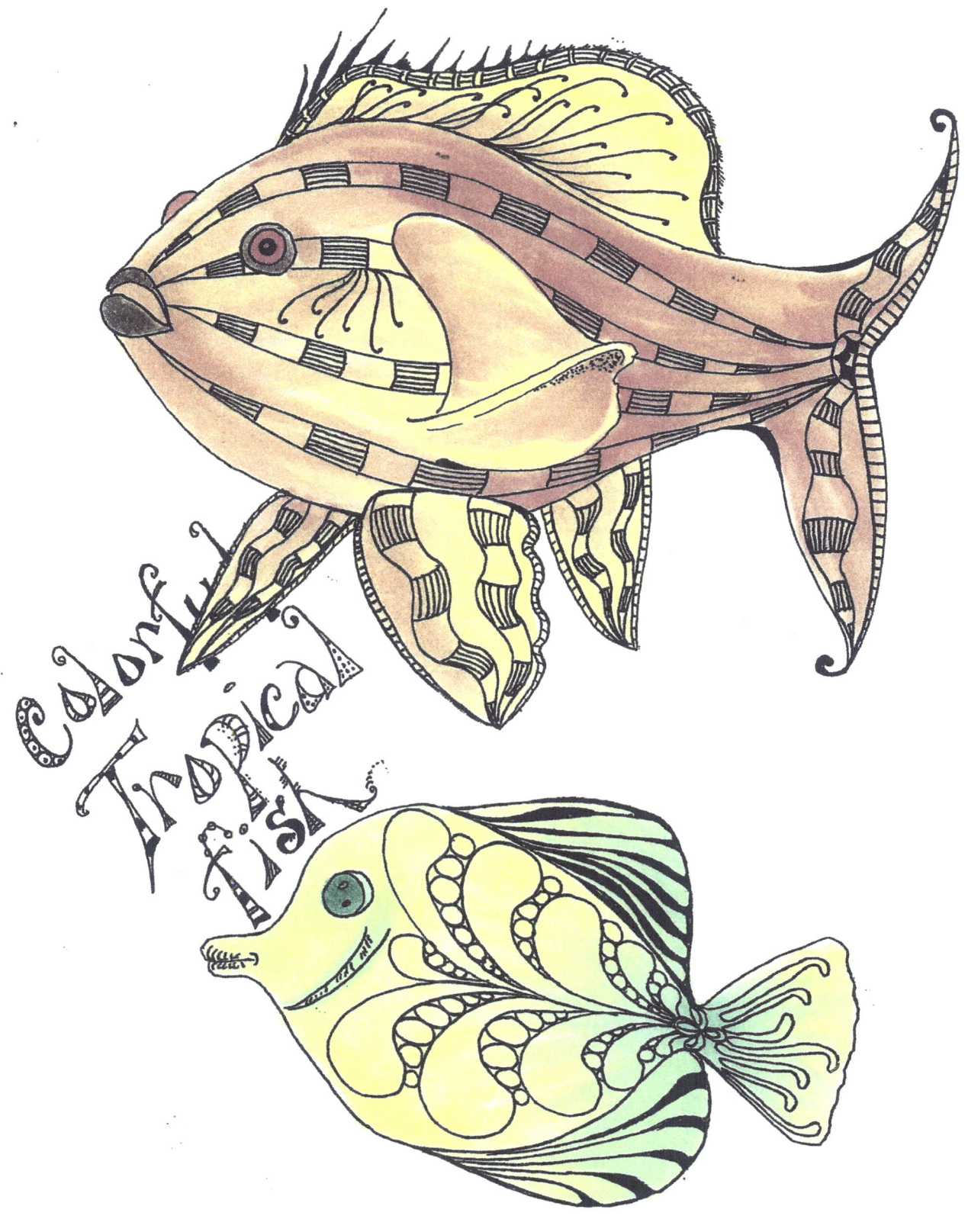

Colorful Tropical Fish

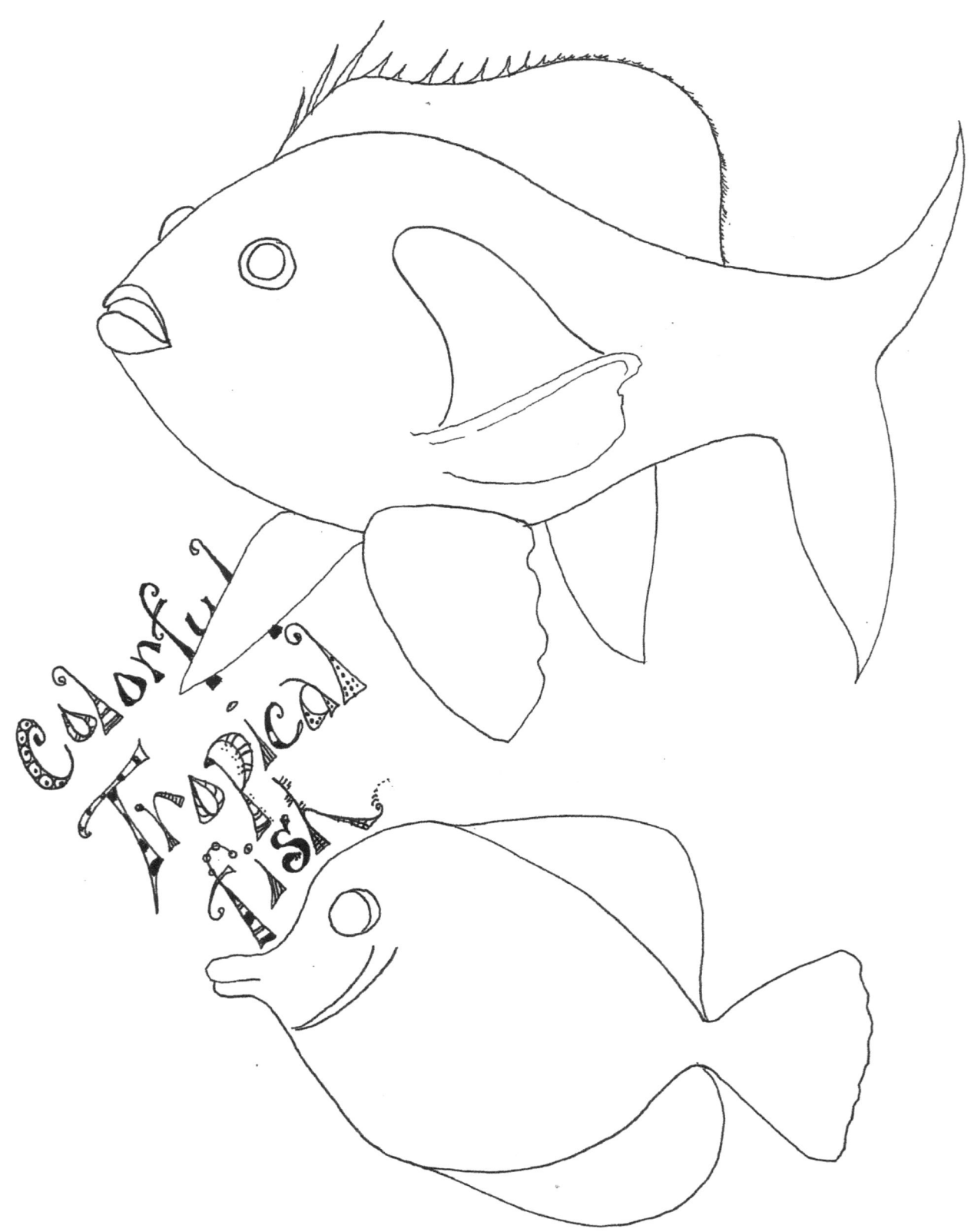

Colorful Tropical Fish

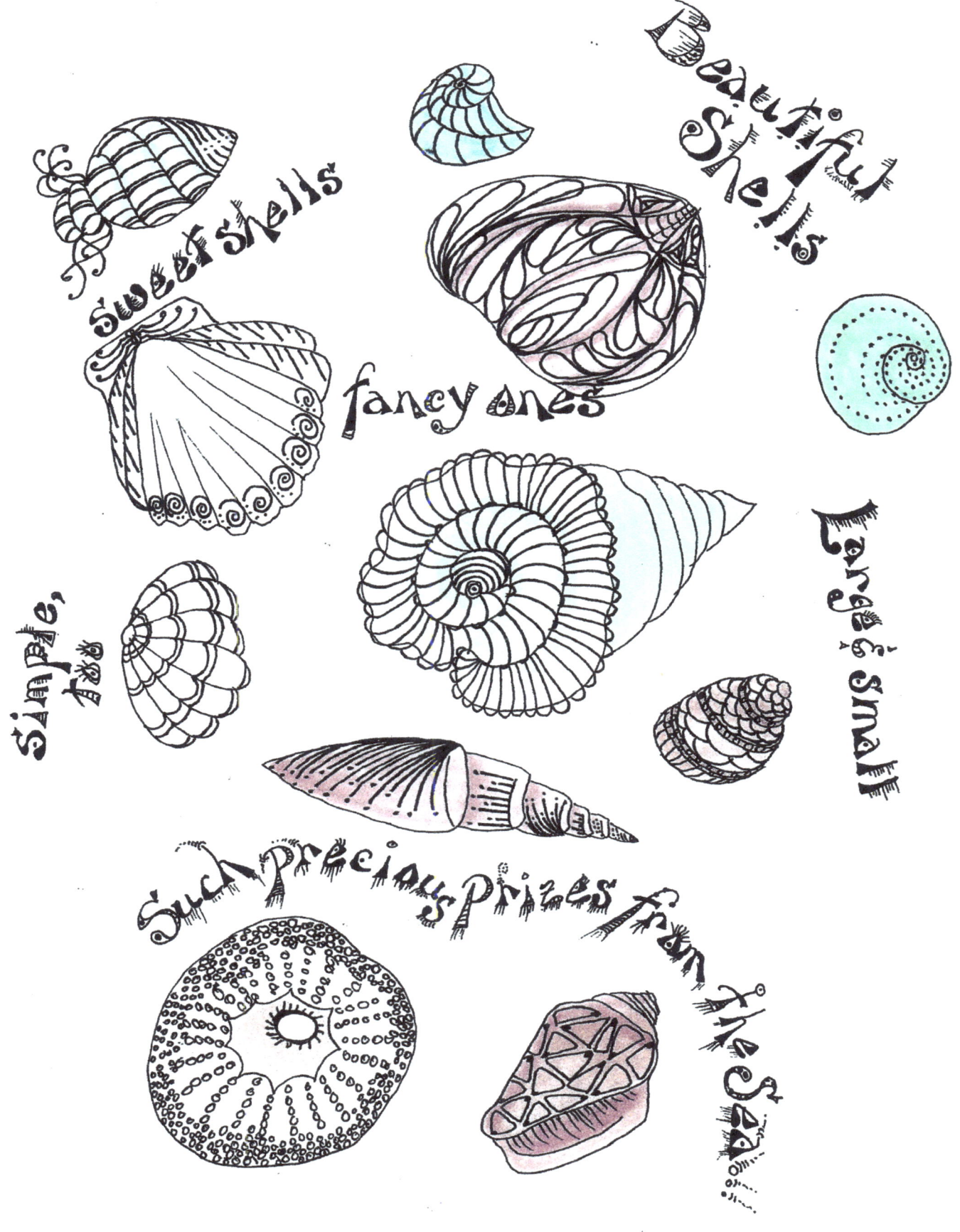

Beautiful Shells

Sweet shells

fancy ones

Simple, too

Large & small

Such precious prizes from the Sea

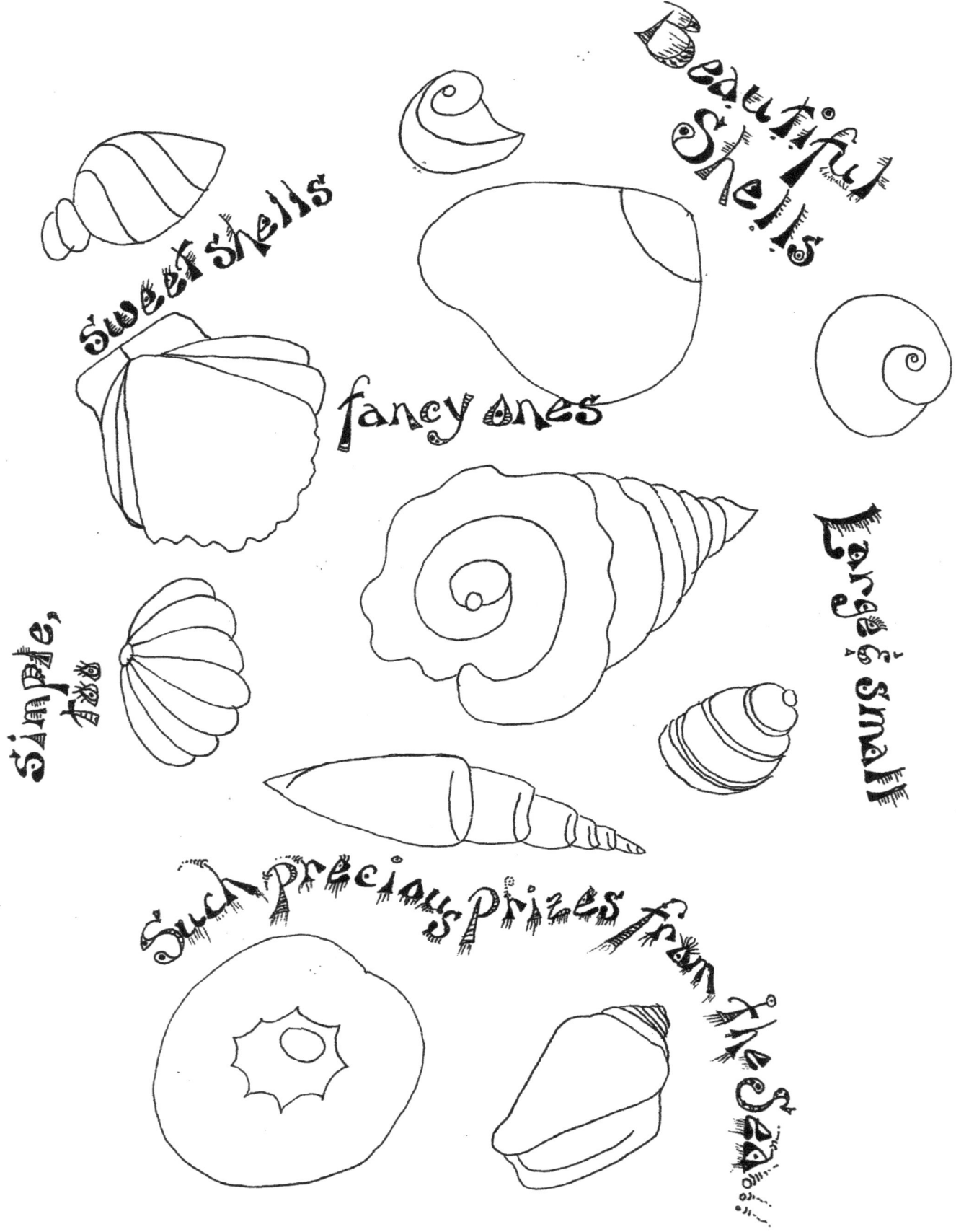

Beautiful Shells

Sweet shells

fancy ones

Large & small

simple, too

Such precious prizes from the Sea

There are plain fish, fancy fish and these tangled fish....

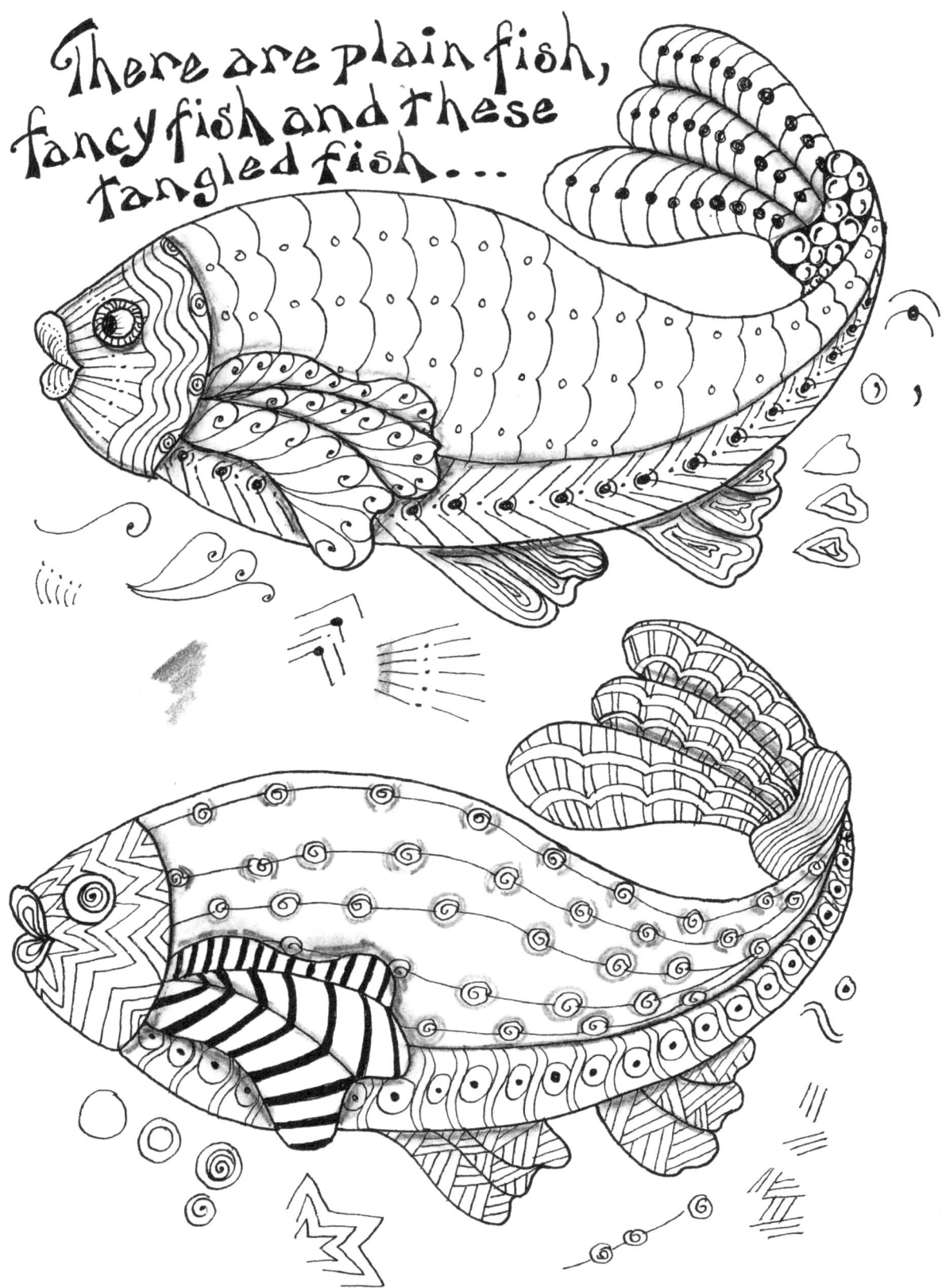

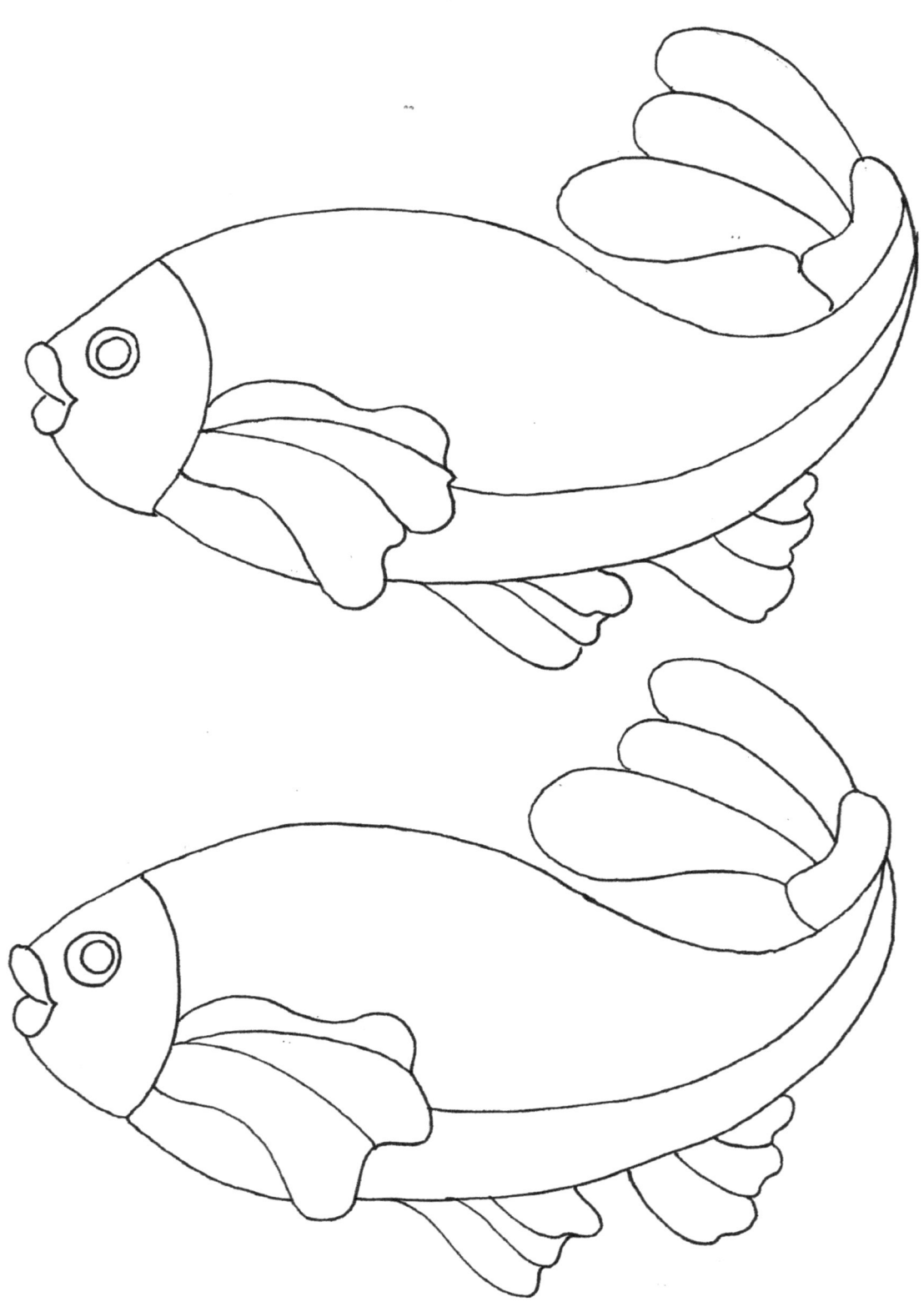

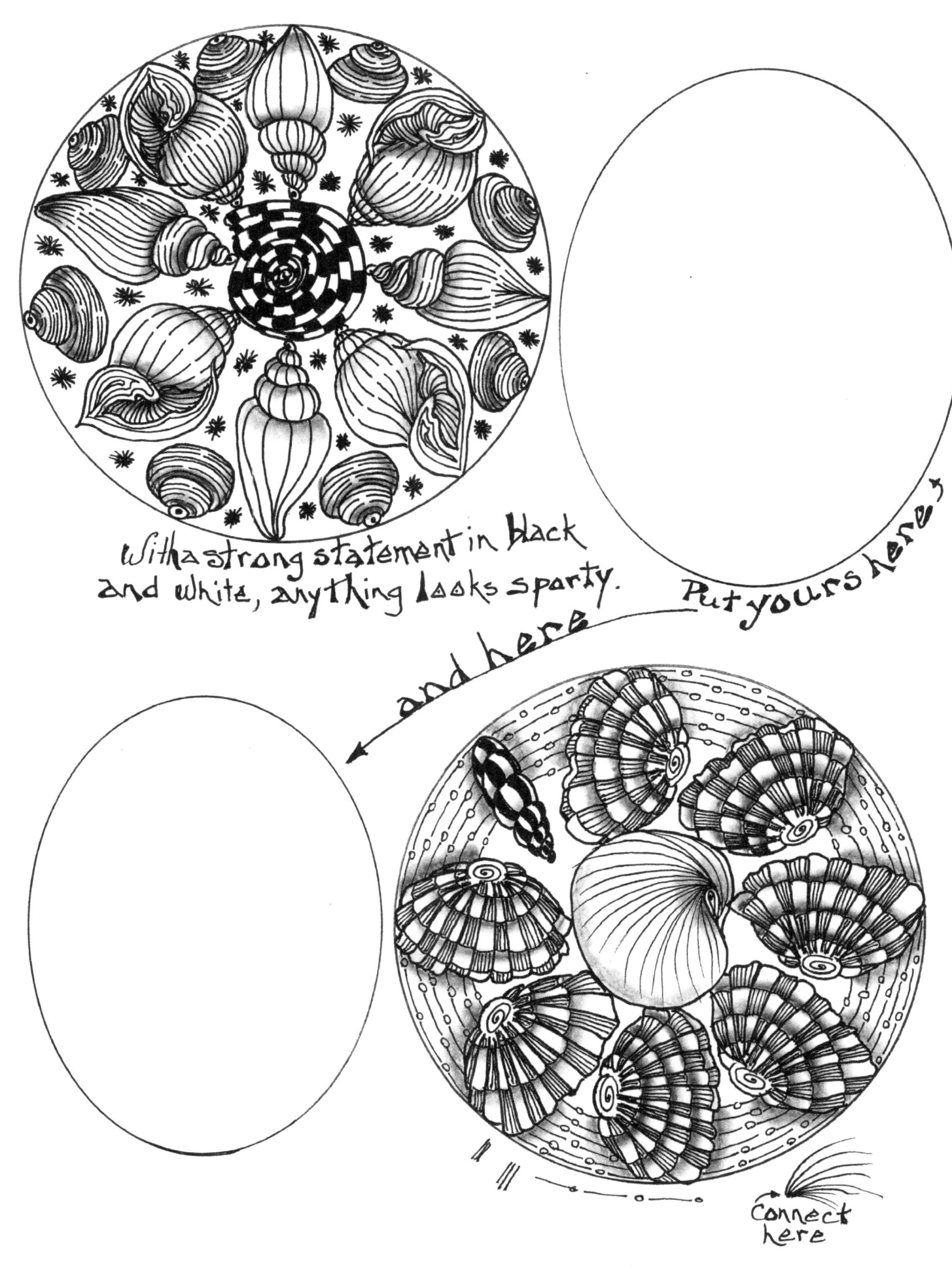

With a strong statement in black and white, anything looks sporty.

Put yours here →

and here

Connect here

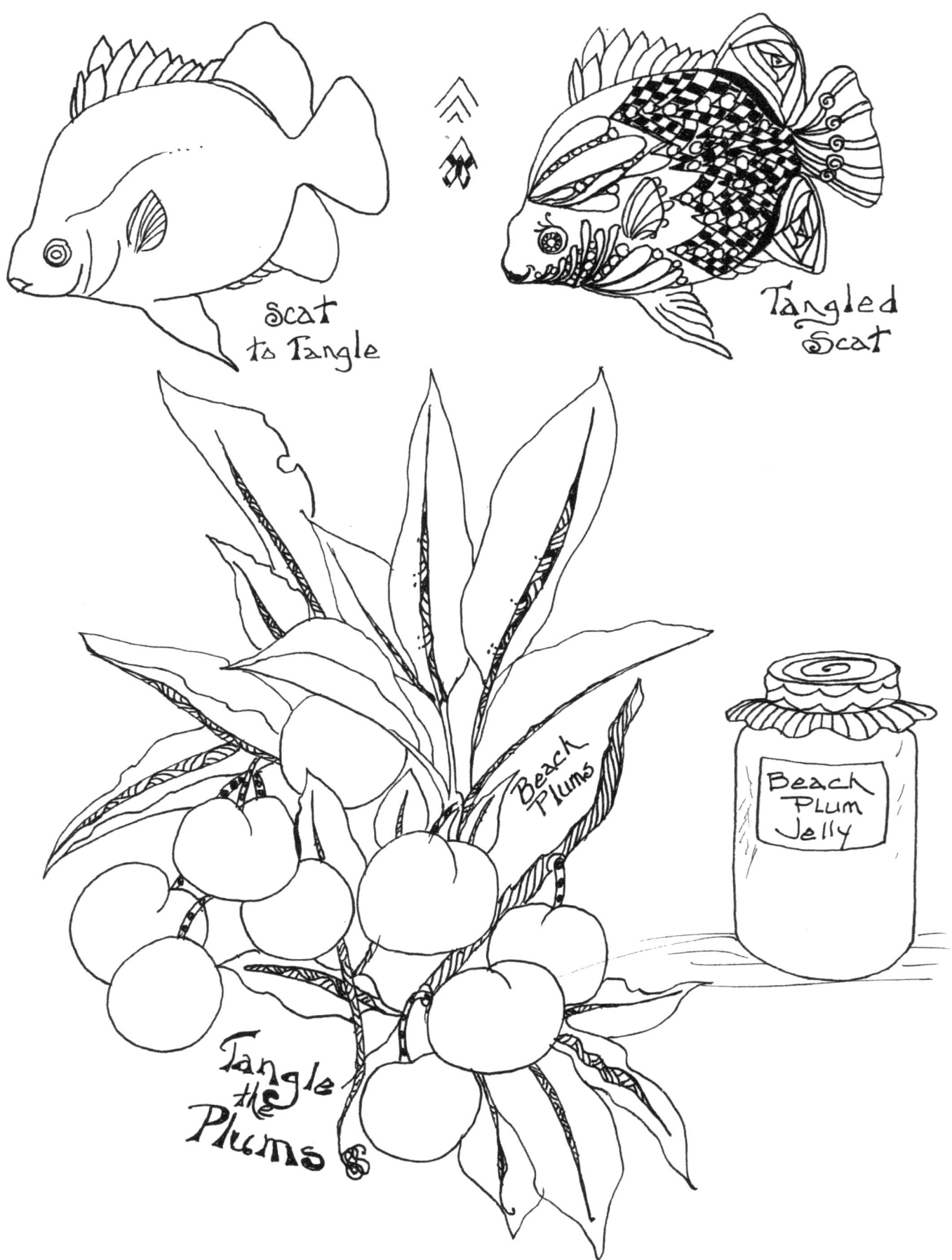

Scat to Tangle

Tangled Scat

Beach Plums

Beach Plum Jelly

Tangle the Plums

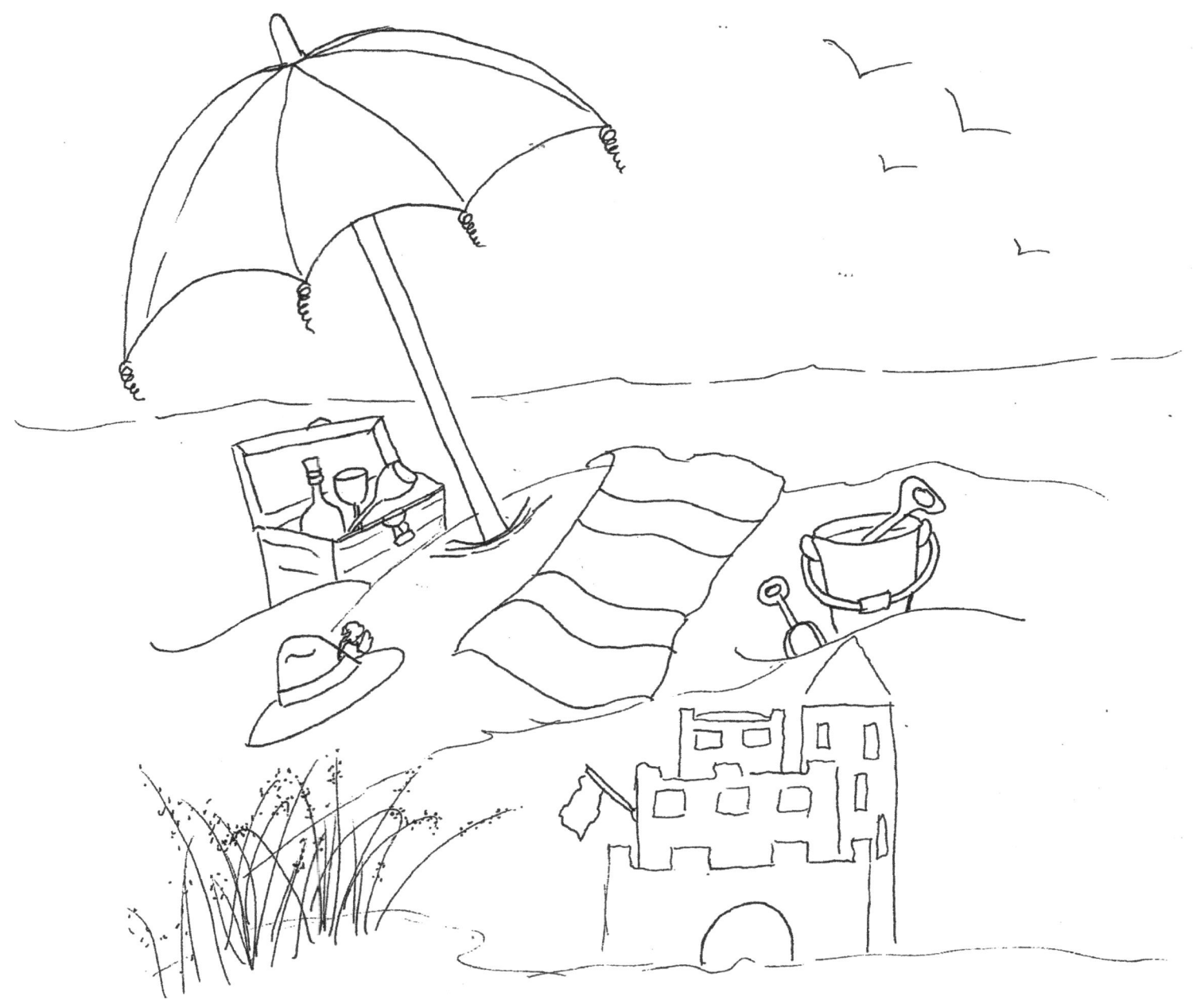

Beach Play

Sea shells, sand castles, ocean blue,
Sunshine, cool breezes, sea gulls, too
Hear the children laugh and shout,
As they play and run about.
(PreKfun.com)

Tangle these lighthouses. Be daring, go ahead, you can do it!

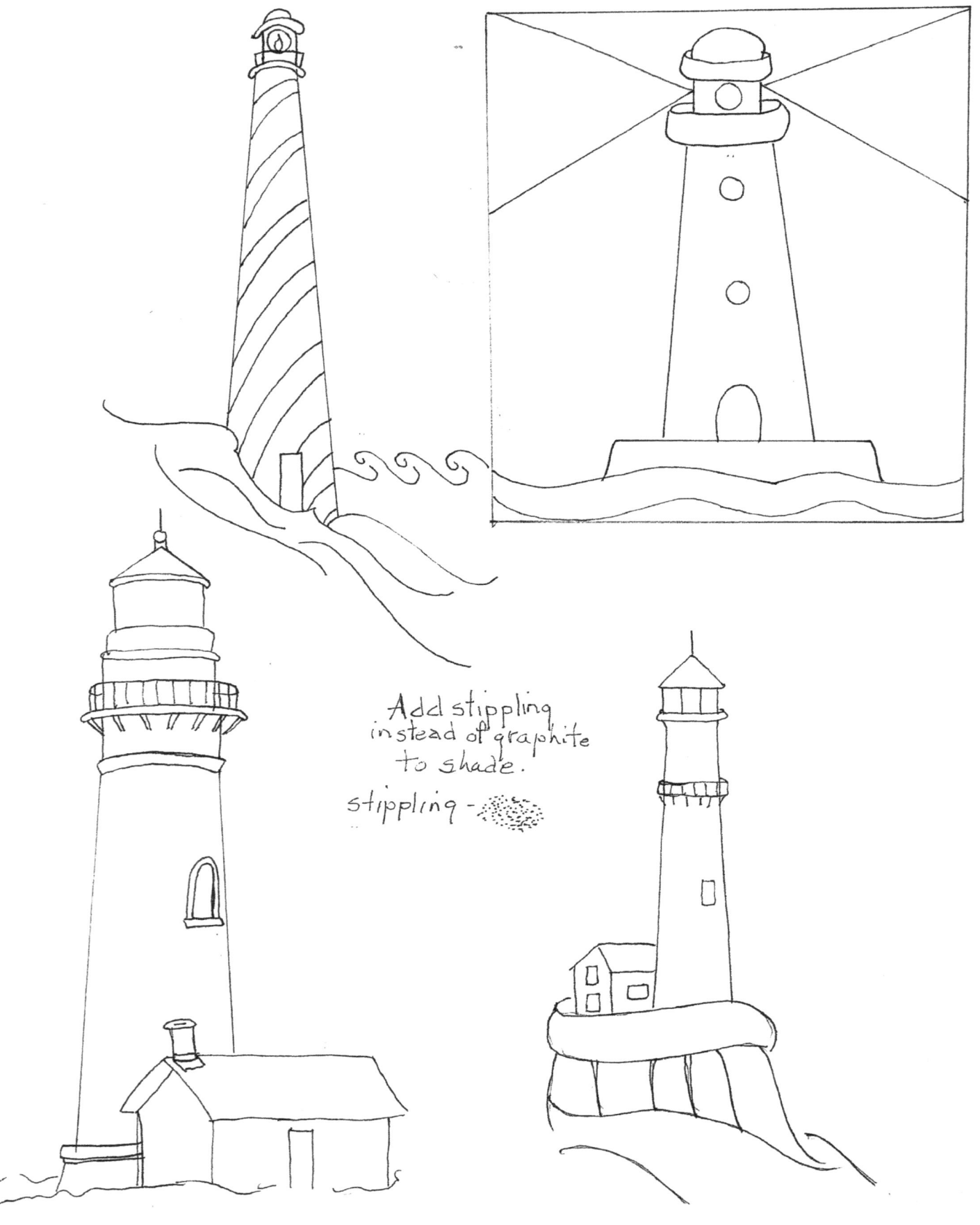

Add stippling
instead of graphite
to shade.

stippling -

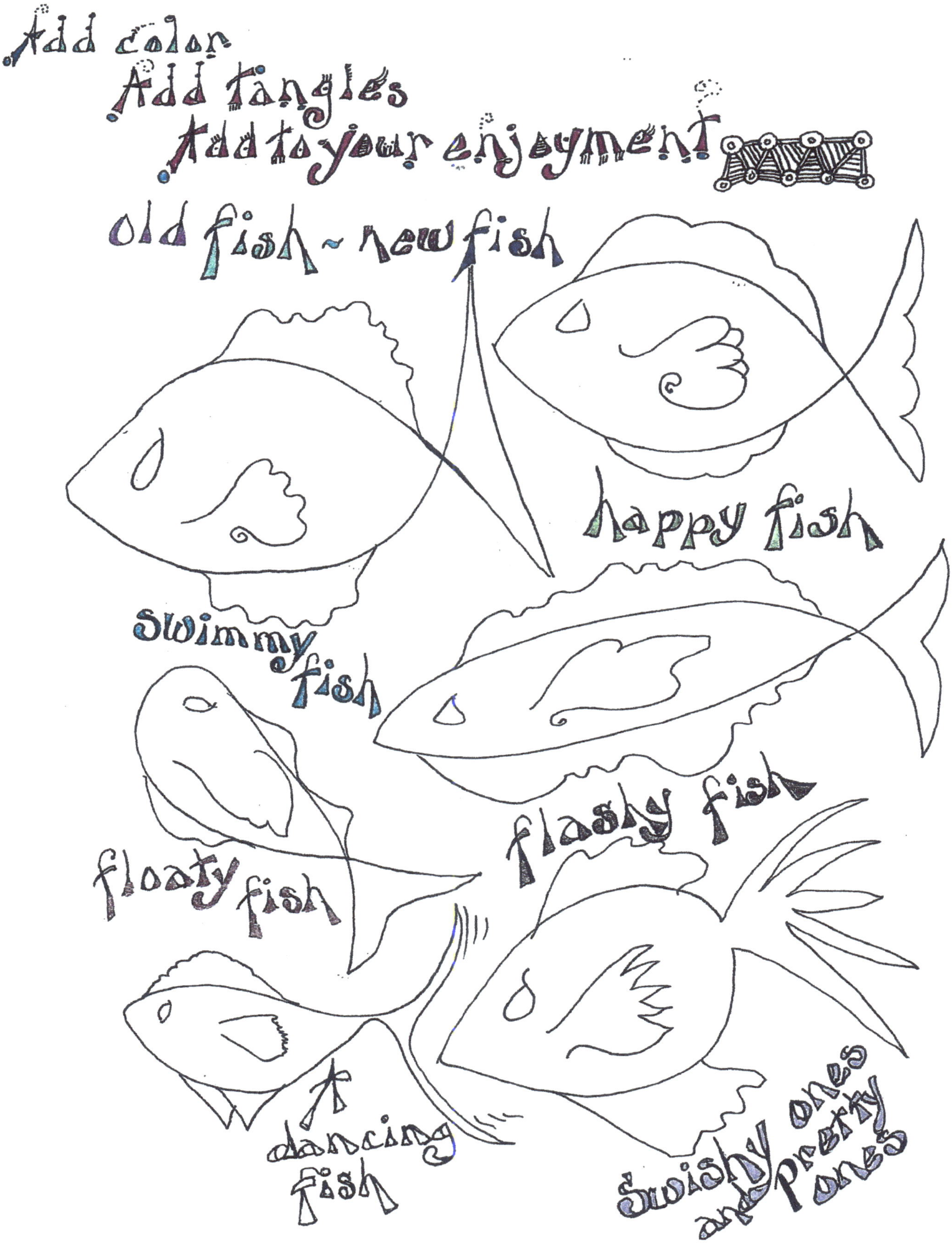

Add color
Add tangles
Add to your enjoyment

old fish ~ new fish

happy fish

swimmy fish

flashy fish

floaty fish

dancing fish

swishy ones and pretty ones

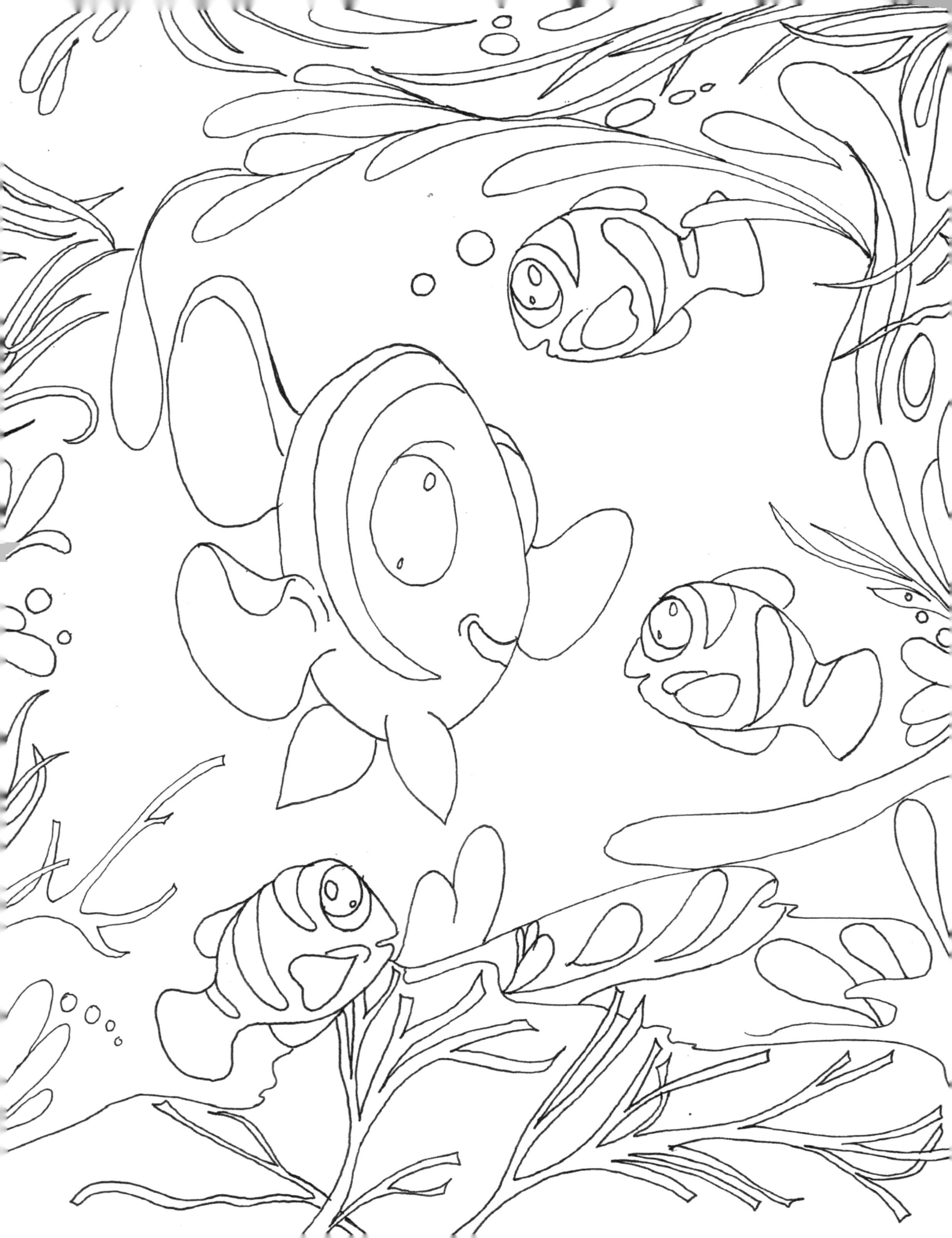

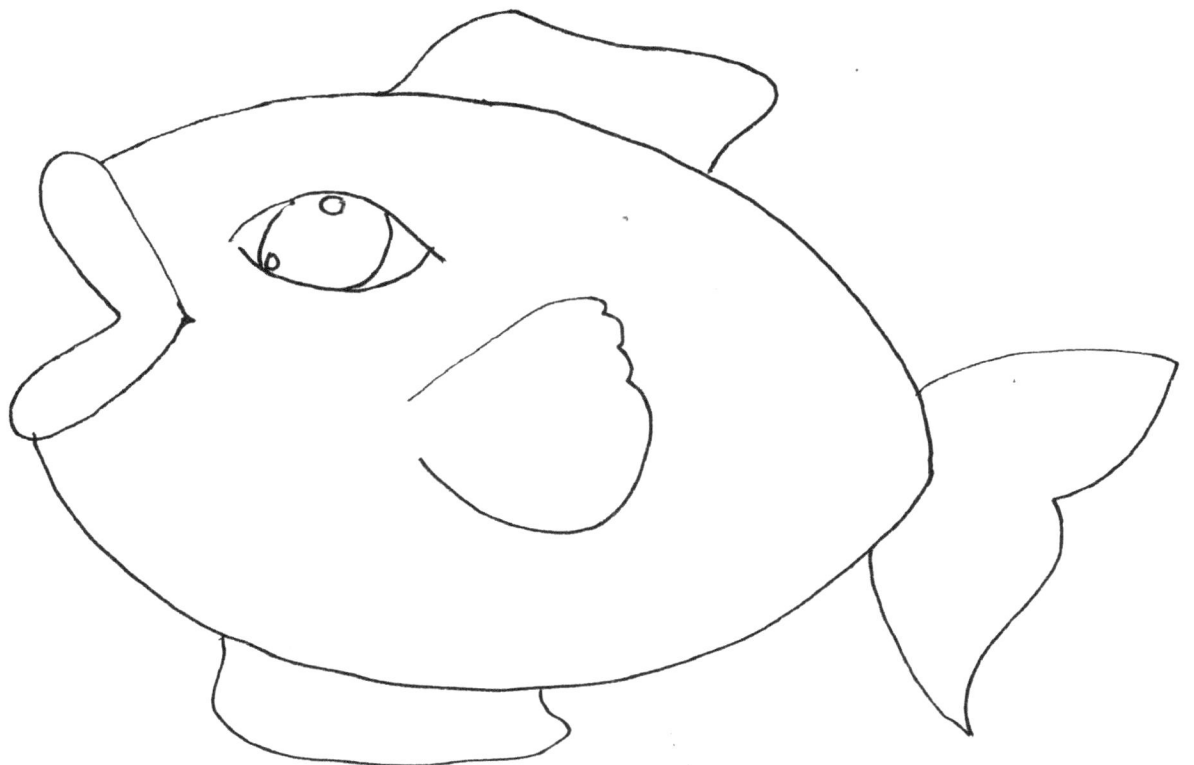

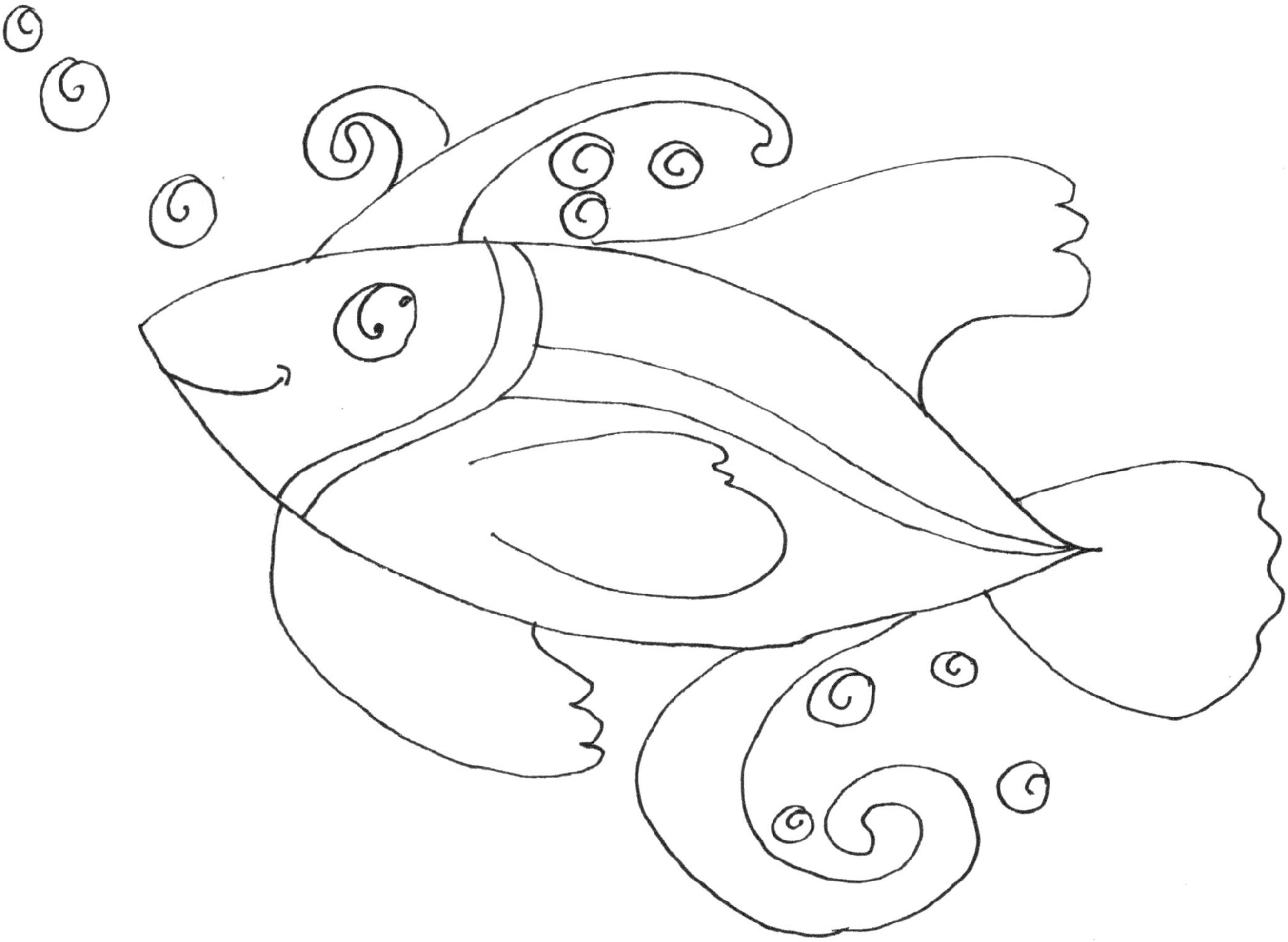

~~~~~~~~~~~~~~~~~~~~~~~~~~~~Swimming Fishes ~~~~~~~~~~~~~~~~~~~~~~~~~

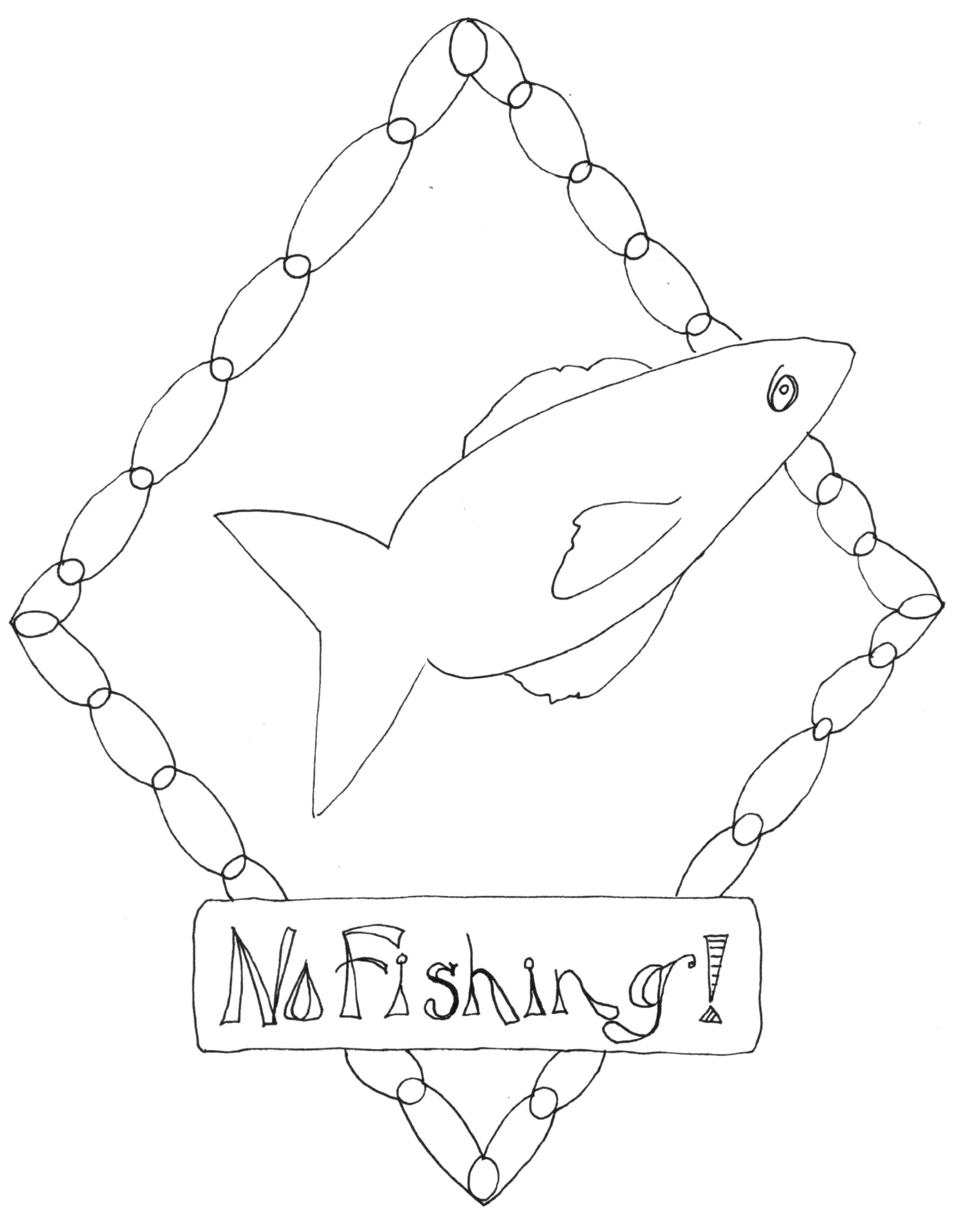

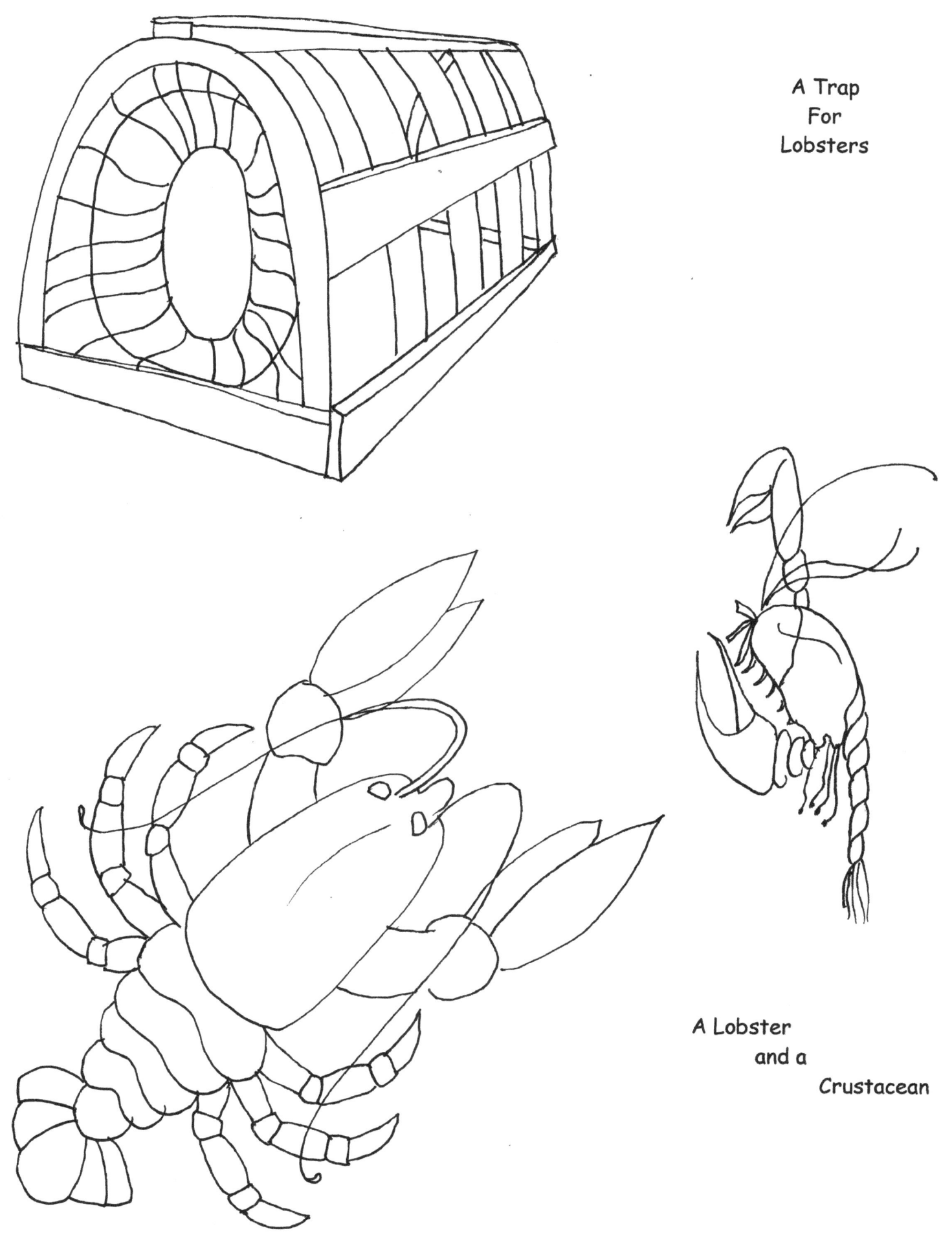

A Trap
For
Lobsters

A Lobster
and a
Crustacean

A Fishing Boat

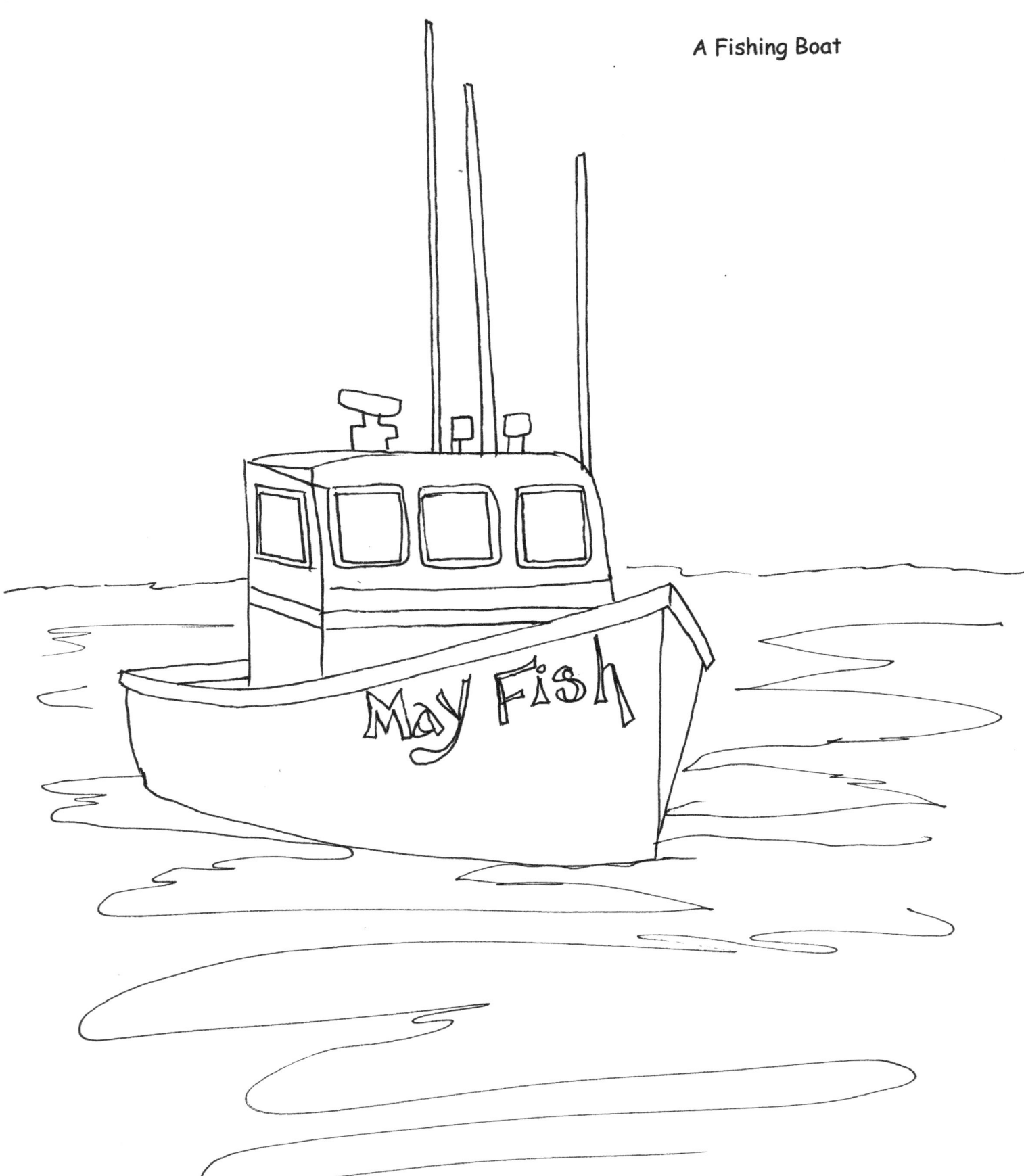

Sunset on the dock

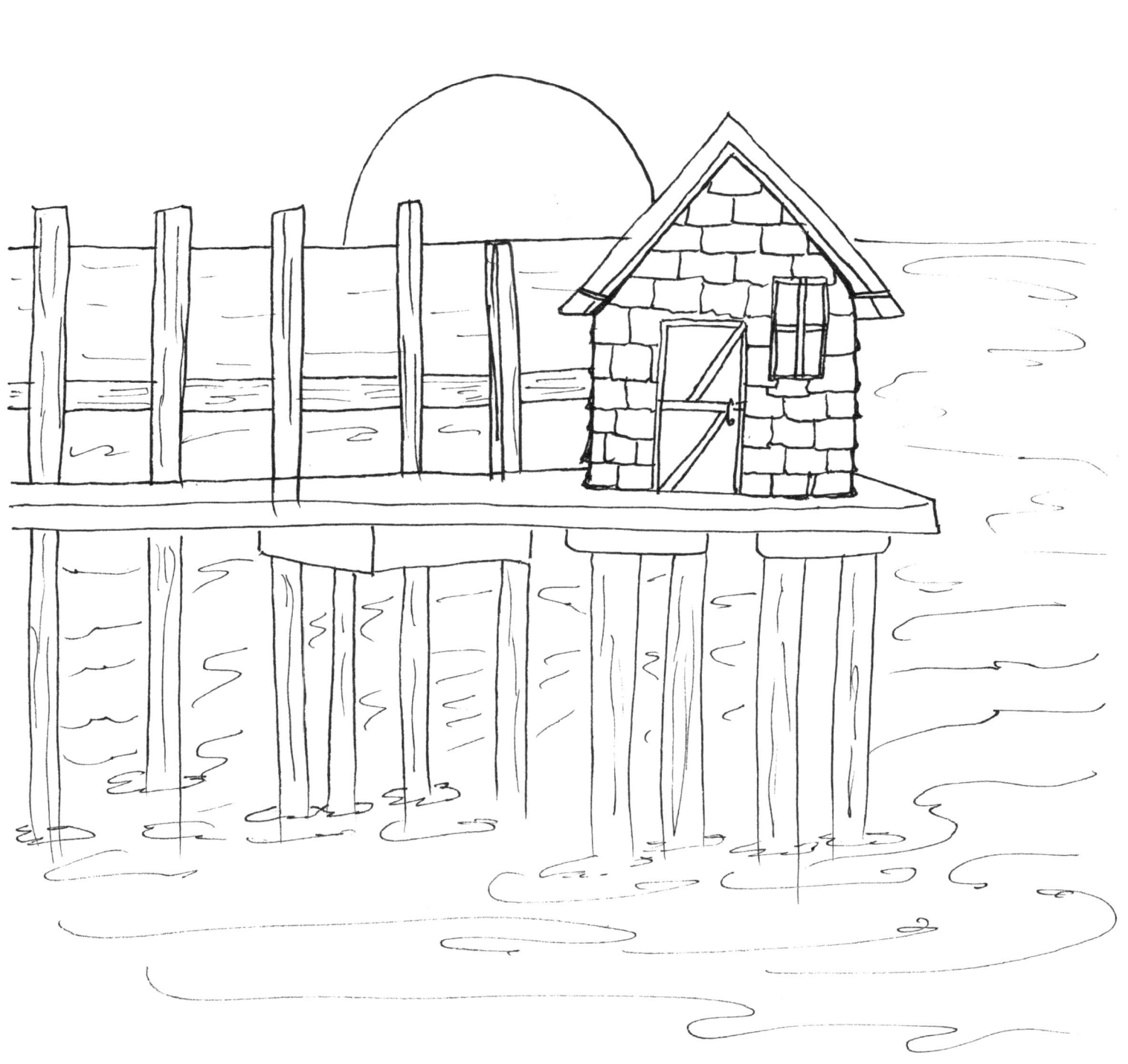

Sunset on the beach

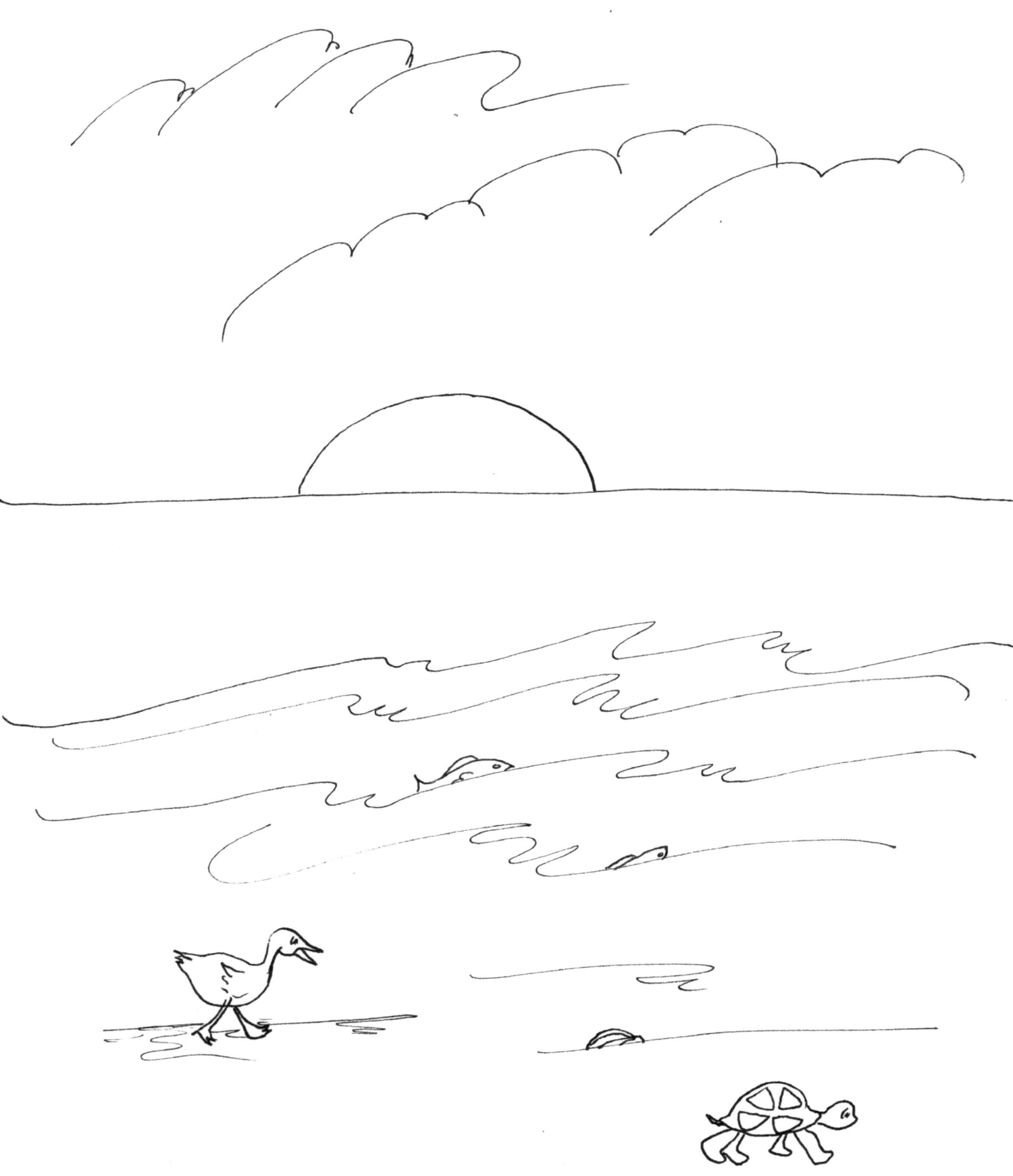

Sunset on the coast line

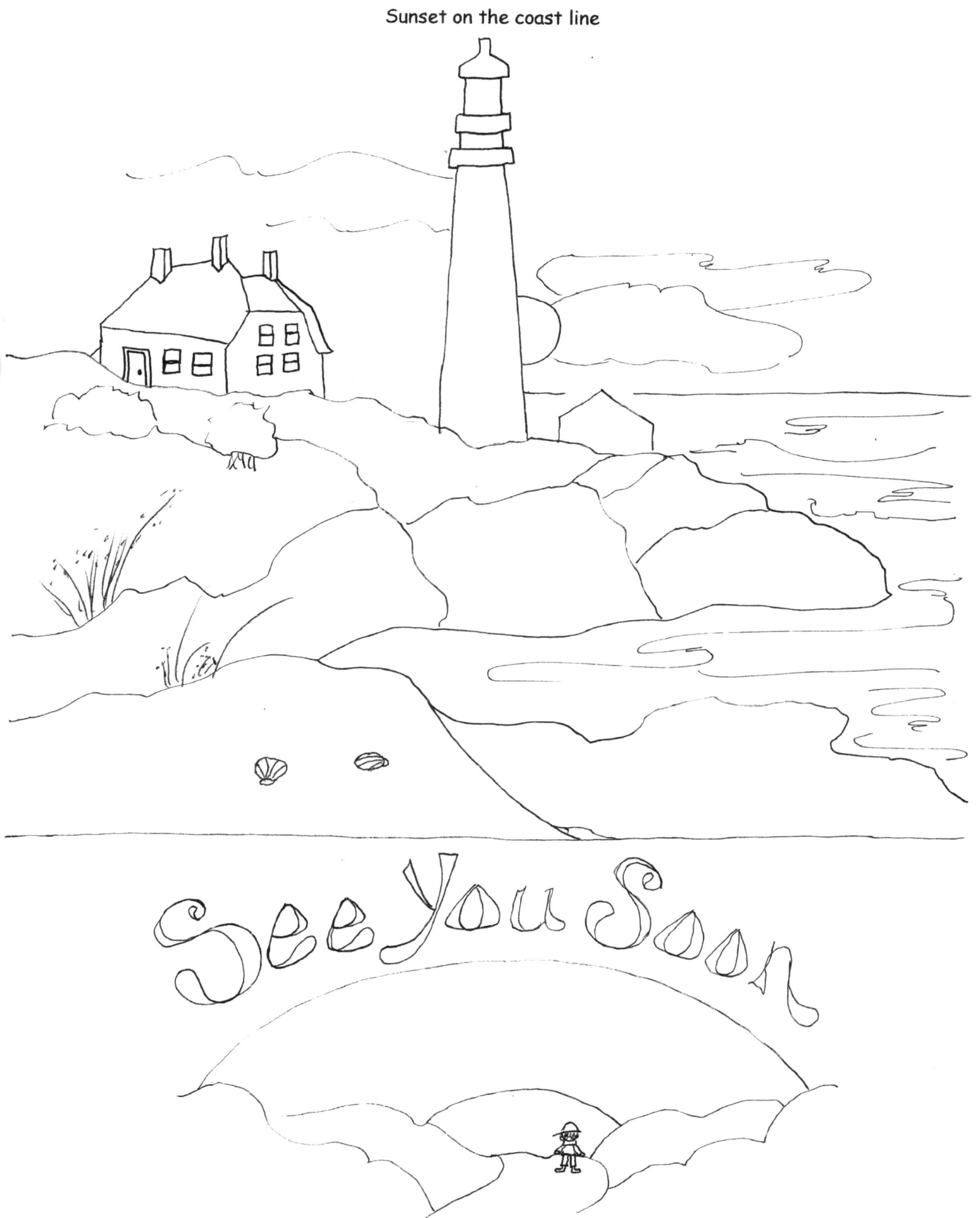